AIR FRYER REVOLUTION

AIR FRYER REVOLUTION

100 CRISPY, HEALTHY, FAST & FRESH RECIPES

URVASHI PITRE

PHOTOGRAPHY BY GHAZALLE BADIOZAMANI

HOUGHTON MIFFLIN HARCOURT

BOSTON   NEW YORK   2019

For information about permission to reproduce selections from this book,
write to trade.permissions@hmhco.com or to Permissions, Houghton Mifflin Harcourt
Publishing Company, 3 Park Avenue, 19th Floor, New York, New York 10016.

hmhbooks.com

Library of Congress Cataloging-in-Publication Data is available.

ISBN 978-0-358-12087-2 (pbk)

ISBN 978-0-358-12303-3 (ebk)

Book design by Jennifer K. Beal Davis

Printed in China

C&C 10 9 8 7 6 5 4 3 2 1

To my father, Brigadier Pitre,
who left us this year. Thank you for everything
you did for me, and for your constant, unwavering
love, even when I was difficult to love.

CONTENTS

① APPETIZERS

② EGGS & CHEESE

7 DESSERTS

8 SPICE MIXES

ACKNOWLEDGMENTS

I am so grateful that my husband Roger and my son Alex support me through my crazy adventures. It's not easy to manage a full-time job, a blog, cookbooks, videos, and culinary tours. It would be impossible without your help.

Thanks to John Kasinger and Diane Mastel for helping me test and finesse the recipes and for your honest feedback. Thanks also for coming willingly to Sunday lunches where we sometimes had nothing but four desserts to taste test!

Ms. Jen Neefer—what a great friend you have been to me over the last crazy year of blogging and cookbooking! Your eagle eye in helping me edit this book will benefits thousands of others.

Thanks to Lisa Kingsley for your excellent thought partnership and help as I worked through this book.

My agent Stacey Glick, thank you so much for your continuing support—and for listening to my "100 ideas in 50 days" type of brainstorming.

My editor, Justin Schwartz, whose lightning-fast responses to emails fit very well with my own work style, and whose honest feedback makes me work harder and do better.

Ghazalle Badiozamani and her team of accomplished stylists and helpers make my food look pretty—not just tasty. Thank you to Monica Pierini, Leila Clifford, Jenna Tedesco, and Bridget Kenny for your great work. I always look forward to our photo shoots, so that I can spend some time with you.

Thanks also to the whole army at Houghton Mifflin Harcourt that helped, without my even realizing it, to make this book a reality.

And of course, to my fans, followers, and readers who continue to support, suggest, encourage, and make me laugh daily. I hope you enjoy this book as much as you seem to enjoy the others.

INTRODUCTION

So you bought yourself that air fryer you've been craving. You've made the obvious things like French fries and breaded foods, and every convenience food you thought would work in the air fryer.

Now what?

Well, now you're about to learn that your air fryer is good for more than just breaded and packaged foods. You're about to see how you can start with fresh ingredients and make delicious, healthy dishes with very little work.

I've tried to create dishes that mostly require about ten minutes of prep, a little time to marinate, and just ten to twenty minutes of actual cook time, most of which is unsupervised. Cakes and frittatas are an exception in that they require longer to cook, but the majority of the main dishes come together with very little effort.

Some of you may look at a few of the ingredients and spices and wonder if you really want to get into cooking Indian, Korean, or Brazilian food at home. Here's what I can tell you: First, yes, you do indeed want to make these simple, flavorful, authentic recipes at home. You can do this. If you can measure, slice, chop, blend, and stir, you can make these recipes. Second, with an air fryer, as with much of cooking, success is all about the spices, marinades, and sauces you use. There are only so many ways you can air fry plain grilled chicken before you tire of it. After that, your air fryer gets less and less of your attention, and soon you've moved on to the next appliance.

Now, I'm all about the next appliance (#GadgetGeek), but if you follow my advice, you'll find your air fryer can be an endless source of varied tastes, a key to using food to open the doors of multiple cultures, and a great way to introduce you and your loved ones to an explosion of flavors.

When I call for unusual ingredients, I try to use each in more than one recipe so you have a few different ways to use them. So don't be afraid to buy a few ingredients that seem new and different and give them a whirl. (If you can buy them in smaller quantities, like in the bulk spices section of your grocery store, that's perfect.)

I hope you enjoy each of the well-tested recipes in this book. But most important, I hope this book equips you with the know-how to make your own tweaks and, ultimately, as you get more comfortable with your air fryer, to feel confident making your own air fryer recipes to enjoy and share.

In fact, my TwoSleevers International Instant Pot, Air Fryer & More Recipes group on Facebook (facebook.com/groups/twosleevers) and my blog (twosleevers.com) are great places for you to come share your food photos, your questions, and your recipe creations. I hope to see you there!

A FEW WORDS ABOUT THE RECIPES

EASY

All the recipes in this book are easy enough that novice cooks can make them, but are so flavorful that even experienced cooks will be proud to serve them. If you can chop, mix, and stir, you can make the recipes in this book.

VERSATILE

I tried to include various cuts of meat (chicken thighs, Cornish game hens, flank steak, meatballs, scallops, shrimp, etc.) so you would have an idea of prep and cooking times for a variety of things. But I also provide a lot of spice and sauce recipes (e.g., ras al hanout, harissa, zhoug, chermoula, etc.). I want to encourage you to mix and match the various meats and vegetables with the different spices and sauces. Once you start doing that, you will find that this cookbook contains a lot more than 100 recipes, and that you will be serving up a constantly rotating series of delightful meals. Definitely check out my first air fryer book (*Every Day Easy Air Fryer*) as it, too, offers many different spice and sauce mixes.

TESTED

If you've followed my blog or are in my Facebook group, you know how much I test and retest recipes. Every recipe in this book was tested. If it doesn't work, it's time to troubleshoot other issues (see page xxiv), because it was likely something other than the recipe that failed you.

USE FRESH FOODS

I prefer to use fresh ingredients rather than prepackaged foods, so much so that this book includes recipes for making your own spice blends. If I use a prepackaged ingredient (e.g., puff pastry), it's because that ingredient is truly complicated for a home cook to make, and because the store-bought equivalent is of good quality.

I also do this when ingredients are not easily found (e.g., myriad ingredients in an authentic Thai curry paste). I use canned tomatoes to provide consistency of flavor and canned coconut milk for ease of use. Other than that, it's mainly fresh meats and vegetables!

MOSTLY HANDS OFF

I absolutely detest recipes that require multiple steps, dirty every dish in the house, and call for three appliances—all so you can have a grilled cheese sandwich. The recipes in this book require minimal prep, may only ask you to flip the food once halfway through cooking, if that, and are almost entirely cooked in the air fryer. If you are mobility impaired, have a fractious child who needs to be held, or would rather check your phone than babysit your food, you will appreciate the ease of the recipes in this book.

NO PREHEATING REQUIRED

I have a confession to make. Never in my years of cooking have I ever preheated an oven for a recipe. And yet, somehow, I have managed to survive and thrive. None of the recipes in this book call for preheating. In addition to my #RuthlessEfficiency approach to cooking, this is in part due to the fact that not all air fryers are equipped for timed preheating. The cook times specified assume you're starting with a cold air fryer.

REQUIRE MINIMAL TWEAKING

I tested these recipes in a GoWISE 3.7-quart air fryer, a Gourmia 5-quart, and a Philips Avance XL, which have very different price points and also differ in wattage. By and large, however, the cook times required for all were quite consistent. Since other air fryers may differ in wattage and capacity, the first few times you make a recipe from this book, I'd suggest you check the food a few minutes before the end of the cooking time, just in case your air fryer is "special."

HOW IS AN AIR FRYER DIFFERENT FROM AN OVEN?

This question comes up a lot. What's the difference between an air fryer, a regular (conduction) oven, and a convection oven? Do you really need all three? An air fryer is mostly a self-contained convection oven with a powerful fan. What differentiates it from a regular oven is that it uses convection rather than conduction to heat food. What differentiates it from a convection oven can be the intensity of the forced fan heat. Here's a quick primer on conduction ovens, convection ovens, and air fryers, and why I like having my air fryer in addition to my oven.

CONDUCTION VS. CONVECTION

Conduction cooking is when cold food heats up via direct contact with a hotter surface or other hot food. You put a pan on the stove. The stove heats the pan. The pan heats the food. You get to eat dinner. This is direct heat transfer from one object to another. Heat flows from a hot object/ surface to a colder object/surface. With convection cooking, not only do you have this type of direct transfer, you have one additional source of heat: hot air. A fan in the oven circulates hot air around the food, resulting in more even cooking. I know you want to make jokes here (or maybe that's just me), but this hot air circulating in the oven touches the surface of the food in the oven and cooks, or "air-fries" the food, resulting in a crisp outer crust. In this case, it is the hot molecules of air that are also cooking your food, not just heat transfer from one object to another.

WHY DOES ANY OF THIS MATTER TO A COOK?

The main reason these things matter is that with convection cooking the circulating hot air is capable of creating a crust of crispiness on the outside of food, which is something we typically associate with fried food. The air in a traditional oven, which is mostly just hanging around, not circulating, can also get humid and create a moist environment. The fan in a convection oven ensures that the air stays relatively dry, once again helping to create crispiness on the outside surfaces of foods while the insides stay moist.

CONVECTION OVENS VS. AIR FRYERS

There are four main differences between a convection oven and an air fryer:

1. **The intensity of the fan.** Depending on your convection oven, it may or may not have as powerful a fan to circulate hot air as an air fryer does. This will affect the crispness of the crust, as explained above.
2. **The size of the oven.** Air fryers are smaller, heat up faster, clean up faster, and may brown and crisp foods better due to their smaller size.
3. **Gentler air circulation for baking.** In a convection oven, the fan-forced air can cause delicate baked goods, such as cakes, to collapse. In an air fryer, the fan is typically at the top and is pulling hot air upward, not creating a tempest of hot air everywhere. I've found that cakes actually bake quite well in the air fryer. Sometimes the fan in your air fryer can leave a brown swirl on top of cakes and cause them to cook unevenly. To counteract this, the recipes

in this book ask you to cover pans of cake batter with foil before baking.
4. **The smaller capacity of an air fryer.** Needless to say, smaller air fryers can't hold as much food as a full-size convection oven. If you tend to make a lot of food at a time, your choices are to stick with a full-size oven, buy an air fryer shaped more like a toaster oven (which will have a larger capacity than an egg-shaped fryer), or cook in batches.

So, do you need both? Many people do have both and report that their air fryer produces much crisper food than their convection oven. For me, the biggest selling point of using an air fryer versus my larger convection oven comes down to ease of cleaning, and the fact that I won't be heating up the whole house. The faster preheat times (2 to 3 minutes for an air fryer versus 20 to 30 minutes for a full-size oven) also speak favorably to my ruthlessly efficient cooking style.

WHY AIR FRY?

HEALTH BENEFITS

The most significant benefit of the air fryer is that it doesn't use nearly as much oil as deep frying. Most recipes in this book call for 1 to 2 tablespoons of oil per pound of meat or 4 cups of vegetables. Depending on the cut of meat you use, you may not need to add any oil at all.

FASTER COOKING

To be precise, the air fryer is 20 to 25 percent faster than a conventional oven. It also requires less energy, as you typically need to set cooking temperatures between 25° and 50°F lower than in an oven. Additionally, most air fryers preheat in 3 to 5 minutes versus the 20 to 30 minutes an oven needs. Note that since not all air fryers have a preheat setting, the recipes in this book do not call for preheating. Just place your food in the air fryer basket, turn on the time and temperature called for, and walk away.

SAFE AND EASY TO USE

If you're really clumsy, like I am, the thought of being around a pot of hot oil is enough to make you break into a cold sweat. The thought of younger family members trying to fry things unsupervised is even more frightening. Air fryers remove these fears entirely.

Typically, air fryers stay cool to the touch on the outside. The air fryer basket itself does get hot, and I did singe myself a little bit a time or two as I was testing recipes, but I still think they're a much safer way for youngsters to learn how to cook than hot stoves, hot oil fryers, or even larger ovens.

EASY TO CLEAN

This, to me, is the clear advantage of air fryers over a full-size convection oven. Most of the parts of the air fryer that come into contact with food are dishwasher-safe. I often hear from people complaining about how much they seem to be scrubbing their baskets. I have a piece of advice for you: Don't. What you need is not elbow grease, but a little patience. I've tried this with five different air fryers: All you need to do is wipe the excess oil and crumbs off the basket with a paper towel and fill

with hot soapy water—and then walk away. Come back 20 minutes later and everything will slide straight off. You can also put the basket into the dishwasher, but it's really a lot faster to wipe, soak, and then rinse.

TROUBLESHOOTING

It's Taking a Lot Longer Than You Say for My Food to Cook

There could be a few different reasons why this is happening. Once you figure out which it is, it will be an easy fix.

- Your air fryer is a different wattage and/or the fan isn't as powerful as the ones in the air fryers I used for testing (a Gourmia 5-quart, a GoWISE 3.7-quart and a Philips Avance XL).
- Your pieces of meat or vegetables are larger than the recipe calls for. The thickness of the food item can drastically affect cook times.
- You're using a deeper cake pan than specified. The thicker the cake/frittata, the longer it will take to cook.
- You're doubling the recipe. The fuller the basket, the longer it will take to cook the food.

The Food Is Partly Cooked and Partly Raw

This can happen if your food isn't in one layer in the air fryer. If you need to double the recipe, I strongly suggest you do so by cooking in two batches rather than trying to put 2 pounds of meat into the air fryer basket, which was not intended to hold that much in one go. Since most of the recipes in this cookbook only cook for 10 to 20 minutes, it's as fast to cook two batches as one overfull batch, and your food will cook more evenly.

My Meat Was Dry Even Though I Followed the Recipe (Oh, but I Did Change the Cut of Meat)

Fattier foods cook better in the air fryer than leaner foods. You can cook lean meats in the air fryer, but you may have to spray with oil more often. For poultry, cuts with the skin on will cook better than skinless pieces. Choose alternate cuts of meat with this in mind. You can definitely substitute your favorite cuts, but if the result is too dry you may need to add more oil, mist with water while cooking, or revert to the specified cut.

There's a Lot of Smoke Coming Out of the Machine as It Cooks

If you see white smoke, that's typically from the fat that has rendered while cooking. You can either stop and pour out the excess fat, or you can add a little bit of water to the container below the basket so the hot fat isn't sitting directly on the bottom of the hot container.

If you see black smoke, that could be a sign your machine is not functioning as it should. Turn it off, call customer service, and do not use the air fryer until they tell you it's okay to do so.

I Don't Understand Why I Spent So Much Money on My Stove When All I Ever Use Are My Instant Pot and Air Fryer

Yup, the struggle is real. Honestly, once you get more familiar with your air fryer, you'll find that you're choosing it over the stove, the grill, and the oven for faster cooking, and over the microwave for reheating food without drying it out. It takes a little tweaking to learn the right temperatures and times, but once you have that down, it's so easy to use your air fryer that you'll wonder how you ever got by without it.

APPET

APP-TIZERS

CHEESE DROPS

These are soft, cheesy, biscuity little bites of heaven. When I first made them, we had a tough time not eating them all before they were photographed. They're great for a party, but you may have to make them at the last minute so you don't eat them all.

SERVINGS: 8 (4 CHEESE DROPS EACH)

1. In a small bowl, combine the flour, salt, cayenne, paprika, pepper, and garlic powder, if using.

2. Using a food processor, cream the butter and cheese until smooth. Gently add the seasoned flour and process until the dough is well combined, smooth, and no longer sticky. (Or make the dough in a stand mixer fitted with the paddle attachment: Cream the butter and cheese on medium speed until smooth, then add the seasoned flour and beat at low speed until smooth.)

3. Divide the dough into 32 equal-size pieces. On a lightly floured surface, roll each piece into a small ball.

4. Spray the air fryer basket with oil spray. Arrange 16 cheese drops in the basket. Set the air fryer to 325°F for 10 minutes, or until drops are just starting to brown. Transfer to a wire rack. Repeat with remaining dough, checking for doneness at 8 minutes.

5. Cool the cheese drops completely on the wire rack. Store in an airtight container until ready to serve, or up to 1 or 2 days.

EGG-FREE, NUT-FREE, SOY-FREE, VEGETARIAN

PREP TIME: 15 MINUTES
COOK TIME: 10 MINUTES PER BATCH
ACTIVE TIME: 15 MINUTES
TOTAL TIME: 35 MINUTES
COOK TEMPERATURE: 325°F

- ¾ cup all-purpose flour
- ½ teaspoon kosher salt
- ¼ teaspoon cayenne pepper
- ¼ teaspoon smoked paprika
- ¼ teaspoon black pepper
- Dash garlic powder (optional)
- ¼ cup butter, softened
- 1 cup shredded sharp cheddar cheese, at room temperature
- Olive oil spray

LEBANESE MUHAMMARA

Every time I bring this walnut-flecked red pepper dip to a party, I have to tell everyone what is in it; but then it's one of the first things to disappear. The combination may sound unusual to some, but the taste will delight you.   SERVINGS: 6

1. Drizzle the peppers with 2 tablespoons of the olive oil and place in the air fryer basket. Set the air fryer to 400°F for 10 minutes.

2. Add the walnuts to the basket, arranging them around the peppers. Set the air fryer to 400°F for 5 minutes.

3. Remove the peppers, seal in a resealable plastic bag, and let rest for 5 to 10 minutes. Transfer the walnuts to a plate and set aside to cool.

4. Place the softened peppers, walnuts, agave, lemon juice, cumin, salt, and ½ teaspoon of the pepper flakes in a food processor and puree until smooth.

5. Transfer the dip to a serving bowl and make an indentation in the middle. Pour the remaining ¼ cup olive oil into the indentation. Garnish the dip with the remaining ½ teaspoon pepper flakes.

6. Serve with vegetables or toasted pita chips.

GRAIN-FREE, GLUTEN-FREE, EGG-FREE, SOY-FREE, DAIRY-FREE, PALEO, VEGAN, LOW-CARB

PREP TIME: 15 MINUTES
COOK TIME: 15 MINUTES
ACTIVE TIME: 15 MINUTES
TOTAL TIME: 30 MINUTES
COOK TEMPERATURE: 400°F

- 2   large red bell peppers
- ¼   cup plus 2 tablespoons extra-virgin olive oil
- 1   cup walnut halves
- 1   tablespoon agave nectar or honey
- 1   teaspoon fresh lemon juice
- 1   teaspoon ground cumin
- 1   teaspoon kosher salt
- 1   teaspoon red pepper flakes

  Raw vegetables (such as cucumber, carrots, zucchini slices, or cauliflower) or toasted pita chips, for serving

MASALA PEANUTS

These seasoned peanuts, typically deep-fried, are a very popular Indian snack. They're super addictive and I tend to shovel them into my mouth mindlessly. Take my advice—put some in a small bowl for yourself before you start eating, otherwise you will look up and find them all gone. You can use any other type of nut you prefer, and amp up or down the spices to your preference. Chickpea flour—also called *besan*—is easily found in Indian markets and whole-foods stores.   **SERVINGS: 4**

PREP TIME: 15 MINUTES

COOK TIME: 15 MINUTES

ACTIVE TIME: 15 MINUTES

STANDING TIME: 10 MINUTES

TOTAL TIME: 40 MINUTES

COOK TEMPERATURE: 325°F/400°F

1. In a medium bowl, combine the chickpea flour, cumin seeds, turmeric, salt, and cayenne. Add the oil and stir to combine. Add the water and stir to make a thick, pancake-like batter. Add the peanuts and stir until well blended.

2. Place a circle of parchment paper in the bottom of the air fryer basket. Pour the peanut mixture onto the parchment paper. Set the air fryer to 325°F for 10 minutes.

3. Open the air fryer and break up the peanuts and batter. Remove the parchment paper and let the peanuts sit directly on the bottom of the air fryer basket. Spray the peanuts generously with the vegetable oil spray. (Don't skip this step or the batter will taste raw.) Set the air fryer to 400°F for 5 minutes, or until the outsides of the peanuts are crisp.

4. Transfer the peanuts to a rimmed baking sheet and shake well. Sprinkle with chaat masala or amchoor, if using. (You can also sprinkle with a little kosher salt.) Let peanuts cool for 10 minutes before serving. (They will continue to crisp as they cool.) Store in an airtight container.

NOTE

★ Amchoor is dried mango powder. Chaat masala is a wonderful mix of magical spices. If you don't have either, just finish it off with generous lashings of lemon or lime juice.

- 5 tablespoons chickpea flour
- ½ teaspoon cumin seeds
- ¼ teaspoon ground turmeric
- ¼ teaspoon kosher salt, plus more for seasoning if desired
- ¼ to ½ teaspoon cayenne pepper
- 2 tablespoons vegetable oil
- 3 tablespoons water
- 1 cup red Spanish peanuts or unsalted roasted peanuts

  Vegetable oil spray

  Prepared chaat masala or amchoor (dried mango powder), optional (see Note)

ONION PAKORAS

This recipe took me three tries to get right. Does it taste exactly like deep-fried pakoras (aka onion bhajis, the tasty savory fritters)? My supertaster mouth says no. Will you care? You will not, because they're delicious anyway. The batter keeps for several days so you could double or triple the batch and let it sit in the fridge until you're ready to make a few to snack on. The rice flour makes them really light and crisp.   **SERVINGS: 2 (6 PAKORAS EACH)**

1. In a large bowl, combine the onions, cilantro, oil, chickpea flour, rice flour, turmeric, cumin seeds, salt, and cayenne. Stir to combine. Cover and let stand for 30 minutes or up to overnight. (This allows the onions to release moisture, creating a batter.) Mix well before using.

2. Spray the air fryer basket generously with vegetable oil spray. Drop half of the batter in 6 heaping tablespoons into the basket. Set the air fryer to 350°F for 8 minutes. Carefully turn the pakoras over and spray with oil spray. Set the air fryer for 2 minutes, or until the batter is cooked through and crisp.

3. Repeat with remaining batter to make 6 more pakoras, checking at 6 minutes for doneness. Serve hot.

GLUTEN-FREE, EGG-FREE, NUT-FREE, SOY-FREE, DAIRY-FREE, VEGAN, LOW-CARB

PREP TIME: 5 MINUTES

STANDING TIME: 30 MINUTES

COOK TIME: 10 MINUTES PER BATCH

ACTIVE TIME: 10 MINUTES

TOTAL TIME: 1 HOUR

COOK TEMPERATURE: 350°F

- 2 medium yellow or white onions, sliced (2 cups)
- ½ cup chopped fresh cilantro
- 2 tablespoons vegetable oil
- 1 tablespoon chickpea flour
- 1 tablespoon rice flour, or 2 tablespoons chickpea flour
- 1 teaspoon ground turmeric
- 1 teaspoon cumin seeds
- 1 teaspoon kosher salt
- ½ teaspoon cayenne pepper
- Vegetable oil spray

PEPPERONI PIZZA DIP

This dip is great with breadsticks, but also very good with celery sticks for a low-carb option. I like the idea of getting all the tasty bits of a pizza without actually having to make a sauce, make a crust, roll it out, assemble the pizza, and clean a dozen different dishes. **SERVINGS: 6**

GRAIN-FREE, GLUTEN-FREE, EGG-FREE, NUT-FREE, SOY-FREE, LOW-CARB

PREP TIME: 10 MINUTES
COOK TIME: 10 MINUTES
ACTIVE TIME: 10 MINUTES
TOTAL TIME: 20 MINUTES
COOK TEMPERATURE: 350°F

1. In a small bowl, combine the cream cheese, ¼ cup of the shredded cheese, the sour cream, Italian seasoning, garlic salt, and onion powder. Stir until smooth and the ingredients are well blended.

2. Spread the mixture in a 6×3-inch round heatproof pan. Top with the pizza sauce, spreading to the edges. Sprinkle with the remaining ½ cup shredded cheese. Arrange the pepperoni slices on top of the cheese. Top with the black olives and green onion.

3. Place the pan in the air fryer basket. Set the air fryer to 350°F for 10 minutes, or until the pepperoni is beginning to brown on the edges and the cheese is bubbly and lightly browned.

4. Let stand for 5 minutes before serving with vegetables, toasted baguette slices, pita chips, or tortilla chips.

6	ounces cream cheese, softened
¾	cup shredded Italian cheese blend
¼	cup sour cream
1½	teaspoons dried Italian seasoning
¼	teaspoon garlic salt
¼	teaspoon onion powder
¾	cup pizza sauce
½	cup sliced miniature pepperoni
¼	cup sliced black olives
1	tablespoon thinly sliced green onion
	Cut-up raw vegetables, toasted baguette slices, pita chips, or tortilla chips, for serving

PIGS IN PUFF-PASTRY BLANKETS

Take my advice: Do not skip the mustard here. It adds a lovely flavor to the finished pigs in blankets. They make great party appetizers and since they reheat well (350°F for 5 minutes), they're good to make ahead of time. They also freeze well once cooked so you can have some in the freezer for unexpected snacking opportunities. Make sure to take out the puff pastry to thaw 2 hours before starting.   **SERVINGS: 8**

NUT-FREE, SOY-FREE

PREP TIME: 15 MINUTES
COOK TIME: 8 MINUTES PER BATCH
ACTIVE TIME: 15 MINUTES
TOTAL TIME: 30 TO 40 MINUTES
COOK TEMPERATURE: 350°F

- 1 sheet frozen puff pastry (half of a 17.25-ounce package)
- All-purpose flour
- ¼ cup coarse-ground Dijon mustard
- 32 fully cooked cocktail sausages
- 1 large egg, beaten
- 2 tablespoons sesame seeds

1. Thaw the puff pastry according to package instructions.

2. Lightly flour a work surface. Roll the pastry to an 18×12-inch rectangle. Spread the mustard over the pastry. Cut the large rectangle lengthwise in half, then cut each smaller rectangle into 16 equal pieces for a total of 32 rectangles, about 2×3 inches each. (You want the rectangles to be just slightly narrower than the sausages themselves so that the ends of the sausages stick out of the pastry.)

3. Place one sausage on a short end of a pastry rectangle and roll up. Moisten the edge of the pastry with a little water if necessary to seal. Use a fork to prick the pastry in one or two places. Repeat to make 32 pigs in blankets. Brush each pastry with beaten egg and sprinkle with sesame seeds.

4. Place half or one-third of the wrapped sausages in the air fryer basket; don't crowd them. Set the air fryer to 350°F for 8 minutes, or until the pastry is golden brown. Repeat to cook the remaining sausages, checking for doneness at 6 minutes.

SAVORY POTATO PATTIES (ALOO TIKKIS)

GRAIN-FREE, GLUTEN-FREE, EGG-FREE, NUT-FREE, SOY-FREE, DAIRY-FREE, VEGAN

PREP TIME: 5 MINUTES
ACTIVE TIME: 5 MINUTES
STANDING TIME: 10 MINUTES
COOK TIME: 10 MINUTES PER BATCH
TOTAL TIME: 35 MINUTES
COOK TEMPERATURE: 400°F

Aloo tikkis (Indian potato croquettes) usually start with boiled potatoes that are formed into patties and fried. But I don't like recipes with two different cook cycles and wanted an easier way to do this. I found that starting with instant potatoes did the trick just perfectly. The end result is crispy, savory, crunchy, and just delicious. Serve the patties with a little tamarind chutney or mint chutney and you're all set. You can easily double or triple this recipe, and leave the rest of the spiced potato dough to cook another day.   **SERVINGS: 2 TO 3 (4 TO 6 PATTIES EACH)**

2/3 cup instant potato flakes

1/4 cup frozen peas and carrots, thawed

2 tablespoons chopped fresh cilantro

1 tablespoon vegetable oil

1/2 teaspoon ground turmeric

1/2 teaspoon cumin seeds

1/4 teaspoon ground cumin

1/2 teaspoon kosher salt

1/4 to 1/2 teaspoon cayenne pepper

2/3 cup hot water

Vegetable oil spray

Cilantro Chutney (page 84), for serving, optional

1. In a medium bowl, combine the potato flakes, peas and carrots, cilantro, oil, turmeric, cumin seeds, ground cumin, salt, and cayenne. Add the hot water and stir gently until the ingredients are well combined. Cover and let stand for 10 minutes.

2. Form the dough into 12 round, flat patties with even edges. Spray the air fryer basket with vegetable oil spray. Arrange half of the patties in the air fryer basket. Set the air fryer to 400°F for 10 minutes. After 5 minutes of cooking time, spray the patties with oil spray. Remove from basket with a flexible spatula.

3. Repeat to cook the remaining patties, checking at 8 minutes for doneness. Serve hot.

SMOKY HAM & CHEESE PARTY BISCUITS

EGG-FREE, NUT-FREE, SOY-FREE

PREP TIME: 20 MINUTES

COOK TIME: 8 MINUTES PER BATCH

ACTIVE TIME: 25 MINUTES

TOTAL TIME: 40 MINUTES

COOK TEMPERATURE: 400°F

It doesn't have to be ham and cheddar: This is a great base biscuit recipe for adding whatever sort of meat or cheese suits your fancy—or in my case, whatever I happen to have in the fridge on any given day! I call them party biscuits because they are festive and—dare I say—a party in your mouth! **SERVINGS: 6 (3 MINI BISCUITS EACH)**

1. **For the biscuits:** In a medium bowl, combine the flour, baking powder, baking soda, paprika, salt, and cayenne. Whisk until well combined. Using a pastry blender, cut the butter into the flour until the mixture resembles the texture of oatmeal. Stir in the ham and cheese. Add the buttermilk and chives. Stir until combined.

2. On a lightly floured surface, roll the dough to a ½-inch thickness. Using a 1½-inch scalloped biscuit cutter, cut out biscuits. Gather the dough scraps and roll again to a ½-inch thickness and cut out biscuits. Repeat until all the dough has been used. (You should get about 18 mini biscuits.)

3. Arrange half (about 9) of the biscuits in the air fryer basket, leaving at least ¾ inch between them. Set the air fryer to 400°F for 8 minutes, or until biscuits are golden brown.

4. **For the topping:** While the biscuits are baking, combine the butter and garlic in a microwave-safe bowl. Microwave on high for 1 minute, or until the butter is melted.

5. Remove the biscuits from the air fryer and, while they are still warm, brush the tops with the garlic butter.

6. Repeat with the remaining dough. (If the butter topping has solidified after the second batch, microwave for a few seconds to melt again.) Serve warm or at room temperature.

For the Biscuits

- 1½ cups all-purpose flour
- 2¼ teaspoons baking powder
- ¼ teaspoon baking soda
- 1 teaspoon smoked paprika
- ½ teaspoon kosher salt
- ⅛ teaspoon cayenne pepper
- 4½ tablespoons cold butter, cut into cubes
- ½ cup finely diced ham
- ¾ cup shredded sharp cheddar cheese
- ½ cup plus 2 tablespoons buttermilk or whole milk
- 2 tablespoons thinly sliced fresh chives

For the Topping

- ¼ cup (½ stick) butter
- 2 cloves garlic, minced

SMOKY SALMON DIP

Bring this to a party and you will be among the most popular people there. Sometimes I serve the dip cold, but the melty cream cheese in the hot dish is just divine. I love the liquid smoke here. If you live outside the United States and can't find it, don't worry about it. There are enough other flavors to still make this dish tasty.   **SERVINGS: 6**

GRAIN-FREE, GLUTEN-FREE, EGG-FREE, SOY-FREE, LOW-CARB

PREP TIME: 10 MINUTES

COOK TIME: 7 MINUTES

ACTIVE TIME: 10 MINUTES

TOTAL TIME: 17 MINUTES

COOK TEMPERATURE: 400°F

1. In a 6×3-inch round heatproof pan, combine the salmon, softened cream cheese, liquid smoke (if using), pecans, ¼ cup of the green onions, and the salt and pepper. Stir until well combined.

2. Place the pan in the air fryer basket. Set the air fryer to 400°F for 7 minutes, or until the cheese melts.

3. Sprinkle with the paprika and top with the remaining ¼ cup green onions. Serve with sliced vegetables, cocktail breads, and/or crackers.

VARIATIONS

- ★ Use leftover cooked salmon instead of the canned salmon.
- ★ Add hot sauce and Worcestershire sauce.
- ★ Try curry powder for a different flavor.
- ★ Add lemon juice for zing.
- ★ Substitute other nuts for the pecans.
- ★ Use sour cream instead of cream cheese.
- ★ Stir in chopped dill and capers after cooking.

1	(6-ounce) can boneless, skinless salmon
8	ounces cream cheese, softened
1	tablespoon liquid smoke (optional)
⅓	cup chopped pecans
½	cup chopped green onions
1	teaspoon kosher salt (or less if the salmon contains salt)
1 to 2	teaspoons black pepper
¼	teaspoon smoked paprika, for garnish
	Cucumber and celery slices, cocktail rye bread, and/or crackers

SMOKY EGGPLANT TAHINI DIP

GRAIN-FREE, GLUTEN-FREE,
EGG-FREE, NUT-FREE,
SOY-FREE, DAIRY-FREE,
PALEO, VEGAN, LOW-CARB

I know tahini isn't traditional in baba ghanoush, but it lends a nutty creaminess to the dip that I just love. You could certainly skip it in favor of the more traditional taste. In either case, you will soon see that using an air fryer for "roasting" eggplant makes so much sense. Less mess, hands off, and no splatters to clean up.   SERVINGS: 6

PREP TIME: 20 MINUTES
COOK TIME: 15 MINUTES
STANDING TIME: 10 MINUTES
ACTIVE TIME: 20 MINUTES
TOTAL TIME: 45 MINUTES
COOK TEMPERATURE: 400°F

1. Rub the eggplant all over with the oil and place in the air fryer basket. Set the air fryer to 400°F for 15 minutes, or until the eggplant's skin is well browned.

2. Place the eggplant in a bowl, cover with foil, and let steam for 10 minutes to finish cooking.

3. Holding the eggplant over the bowl, remove the skin and discard. Mash the eggplant along with the juices. Add the garlic, tahini, and salt and mix well.

4. Scrape the dip into a bowl. Create a well in the dip using the back of a spoon. Pour the olive oil into the well. Top with paprika and chopped parsley.

5. Serve with vegetables or pita bread.

- 1 large eggplant
- 2 tablespoons olive oil
- 5 cloves garlic, minced
- 2 tablespoons tahini (sesame paste)
- ½ teaspoon kosher salt
- 1 tablespoon extra-virgin olive oil
- ½ teaspoon smoked paprika
- 2 tablespoons chopped fresh parsley
- Raw vegetables and/or pita bread, for serving

EGGS & C

HEESE

CHEESY BAKED GRITS

GLUTEN-FREE, NUT-FREE,
SOY-FREE, VEGETARIAN

Every recipe for baked cheese grits asks you to cook the grits first. Too much work for lazy me! I tried using instant grits and just trusted that they would cook well in the 12 minutes it takes for this recipe—and they sure enough did. #RuthlessEfficiency *and* a tasty dish that you can whip up quickly. Feel free to add some chopped green onions or a few chopped jalapeños for a change of pace. **SERVINGS: 6**

PREP TIME: 10 MINUTES

COOK TIME: 12 MINUTES

ACTIVE TIME: 10 MINUTES

TOTAL TIME: 22 MINUTES

COOK TEMPERATURE: 400°F

- ¾ cup hot water
- 2 (1-ounce) packages instant grits (⅔ cup)
- 1 large egg, beaten
- 1 tablespoon butter, melted
- 2 cloves garlic, minced
- ½ to 1 teaspoon red pepper flakes
- 1 cup shredded cheddar cheese or jalapeño Jack cheese

1. In a 6×3-inch round heatproof pan, combine the water, grits, egg, butter, garlic, and red pepper flakes. Stir until well combined. Stir in the shredded cheese. (The mixture will appear soupy.)

2. Place the pan in the air fryer basket. Set the air fryer to 400°F for 12 minutes, or until the grits have cooked through and a knife inserted near the center comes out clean.

3. Let stand for 5 minutes before serving.

HARISSA SHAKSHUKA

Traditional shakshuka—or eggs in purgatory, as it is sometimes called—requires a separate step for making a spicy tomato sauce. While I'm all in favor of spicy tomato sauce, I'm not so much in favor of the extra steps and dishes. I also like to show you different ways of using one spice mix. So, in this case, I used a harissa paste to shortcut the sauce. Canned tomatoes also help the dish come together quickly. Don't skip the foil wrap—unless you actually like your egg whites half-cooked and half-runny. (It took me three tries to get that right!) **SERVINGS: 4**

GRAIN-FREE,
GLUTEN-FREE, NUT-FREE,
SOY-FREE, DAIRY-FREE,
PALEO, VEGETARIAN,
LOW-CARB

PREP TIME: 15 MINUTES
COOK TIME: 15 MINUTES
ACTIVE TIME: 15 MINUTES
TOTAL TIME: 30 MINUTES
COOK TEMPERATURE: 350°F

1. **For the harissa:** In a medium microwave-safe bowl, combine all the ingredients. Microwave on high for 1 minute, stirring halfway through the cooking time. (You can also heat this on the stovetop until the oil is hot and bubbling. Or, if you must use your air fryer for everything, cook in the air fryer at 350°F for 5 to 6 minutes, or until the paste is heated through.)

2. **For the shakshuka:** In a 6×3-inch round heatproof pan, combine the tomatoes with 1 teaspoon of the harissa and stir until well combined. Taste and add more harissa if you want the sauce to be spicier.

3. Carefully crack the eggs into the tomato mixture, taking care to not break the yolks. Cover the pan with foil and place in the air fryer basket. Set the air fryer to 350°F for 15 minutes. Remove the foil. For a runny yolk, cook for an additional 3 minutes; for a more set yolk, cook an additional 5 minutes.

4. Garnish with fresh parsley and black pepper, if desired.

NOTE

★ This makes about ½ cup harissa. Store leftover paste in an airtight container in the refrigerator for up to 1 month.

For the Harissa

- ½ cup olive oil
- 6 cloves garlic, minced
- 2 tablespoons smoked paprika
- 1 tablespoon ground coriander
- 1 tablespoon ground cumin
- 1 teaspoon ground caraway
- 1 teaspoon kosher salt
- ½ to 1 teaspoon cayenne pepper

For the Shakshuka

- 1 cup canned diced tomatoes with their liquid
- 4 large eggs
- Chopped fresh parsley (optional)
- Black pepper (optional)

SWEET & SAVORY TRIANGLES

EGG-FREE, NUT-FREE, SOY-FREE

I love the idea of getting two different tastes out of one dish. You could serve these little pastries as a dessert or as an appetizer or snack. You can use any sweet or savory preserve, including chutney or jam. And of course, feel free to use salami, capicola, or any other deli meat instead of prosciutto. Microwaving the goat cheese on 50 percent power for 30 to 45 seconds may help it spread more easily. Make sure to thaw the puff pastry two hours ahead. **SERVINGS: 4 (4 PASTRIES EACH)**

PREP TIME: 15 MINUTES

COOK TIME: 10 MINUTES PER BATCH

ACTIVE TIME: 15 MINUTES

TOTAL TIME: 35 MINUTES

COOK TEMPERATURE: 400°F

All-purpose flour

1 sheet puff pastry (half of a 17.3-ounce package), thawed

1/3 cup marmalade or other preserves

4 ounces goat cheese, softened

4 slices prosciutto, each cut into four pieces

1. Lightly flour a work surface. Roll out the thawed puff pastry sheet to a 12-inch square. Using a pizza cutter, cut the pastry into sixteen 3-inch squares.

2. Top each square with a bit of marmalade, a few crumbles of goat cheese, and a piece of prosciutto. Fold the pastry over the filling to form triangles, pressing the edges with a fork to seal.

3. Arrange 8 triangles in the air fryer basket, leaving as much space as possible between them. Set the air fryer to 400°F for 10 minutes, or until the pastry is golden brown. Transfer the finished pastries to a serving plate. Repeat to cook the remaining pastry triangles, checking for doneness at 8 minutes. Serve warm.

TOAD IN THE HOLE

Funny name, great dish. It's basically sausage cooked in a savory batter. This is my shortcut version. I love that all you have to do is add a salad and you've got yourself a meal.　　**SERVINGS: 4**

NUT-FREE, SOY-FREE

PREP TIME: 10 MINUTES
COOK TIME: 35 MINUTES
ACTIVE TIME: 10 MINUTES
TOTAL TIME: 45 MINUTES
COOK TEMPERATURE: 400°F/350°F

1. In a medium bowl, whisk together the flour, salt, and pepper. Make a well in the middle. In a separate medium bowl, combine the eggs, milk, and mustard and whisk until well blended. Slowly whisk the egg mixture into the flour. (You want a batter that's about as thick as pancake batter. If it's too thick, add a little water or additional milk.) Cover the batter and let it rest while you cook the sausages.

2. Pour the oil into a 6×3-inch round heatproof pan. Cut the sausages in half and place in the pan. Place the pan in the air fryer basket. Set the air fryer to 400°F for 15 minutes.

3. Carefully pour the batter on top of the sausages. Set the air fryer to 350°F for 20 minutes, or until the batter has puffed up and is browned on top. Cut into 4 wedges and serve hot.

½　cup all-purpose flour

½　teaspoon kosher salt

½　teaspoon black pepper

4　large eggs

1　cup whole milk

2　tablespoons Dijon mustard

2　tablespoons vegetable oil

4　uncooked pork sausages (about 4 ounces each)

CHEESY HAM & POTATOES RACLETTE

GRAIN-FREE, GLUTEN-FREE, EGG-FREE, NUT-FREE, SOY-FREE

Calling this a "raclette" may be stretching it a bit (see Note), but it was definitely raclette-inspired. Ham, cheese, and potatoes all cooked together to make creamy, gooey, savory dish? Sign me up!   **SERVINGS: 6**

PREP TIME: 10 MINUTES

COOK TIME: 25 MINUTES

ACTIVE TIME: 10 MINUTES

TOTAL TIME: 35 MINUTES

COOK TEMPERATURE: 400°F

1. In a medium bowl, combine the potatoes, onion, ham, paprika, salt, pepper, and oil. Stir until the ingredients are well blended. Transfer to the air fryer basket.

2. Set the air fryer at 400°F for 20 minutes, or until the potatoes are almost tender, shaking once halfway through the cooking time.

3. Transfer the potatoes and onion to a 6×3-inch round heatproof pan. Add the gherkins and stir to combine. Top with the cheese. Set the air fryer to 400°F for 5 minutes, or until the cheese has melted.

NOTE

★ What is raclette, you ask? It's a Swiss specialty in which a semi-hard cheese is melted on tabletop grill and then scraped over cubes of bread, vegetables, cornichons, and charcuterie. Delicious!

8 to 10	baby potatoes, halved (2 cups)
1	medium onion, cut into ½-inch slices
1	cup diced cooked ham
½	teaspoon smoked paprika
1	teaspoon kosher salt
½	teaspoon black pepper
2	tablespoons olive oil
½	cup whole small pickled gherkins or cornichons, cut into bite-size pieces
1	cup shredded Gruyère or Swiss cheese

VEGET

ABLES

BLISTERED SHISHITO PEPPERS WITH SOUR CREAM DIPPING SAUCE

GRAIN-FREE, GLUTEN-FREE,
EGG-FREE, NUT-FREE,
SOY-FREE, DAIRY-FREE,
VEGETARIAN, LOW-CARB

I love the air fryer for roasting vegetables. It's fast, it's mess-free, and the vegetables are typically evenly roasted without having to fuss with them. These small, mildly hot peppers are no exception. If you can't find them, use colorful mini peppers and then enjoy a healthy little treat with the sour cream dipping sauce. Don't forget to use that delicious sauce with absolutely everything else you can think of! Omit the sauce to make this dairy-free.   **SERVINGS: 4**

PREP TIME: 5 MINUTES

COOK TIME: 6 MINUTES

ACTIVE TIME: 5 MINUTES

TOTAL TIME: 11 MINUTES

COOK TEMPERATURE: 400°F

1. **For the dipping sauce:** In a small bowl, stir all the ingredients to combine. Cover and refrigerate until serving time.

2. **For the peppers:** In a medium bowl, toss the peppers with the vegetable oil. Place the peppers in the air fryer basket. Set the air fryer to 400°F for 6 minutes, or until peppers are lightly charred in spots, stirring the peppers halfway through the cooking time.

3. Transfer the peppers to a serving bowl. Drizzle with the sesame oil and toss to coat. Season to taste with salt and pepper. Sprinkle with the red pepper, if using, and the sesame seeds and toss again.

4. Serve immediately with the dipping sauce.

For the Dipping Sauce

- 1 cup sour cream
- 2 tablespoons fresh lemon juice
- 1 clove garlic, minced
- 1 green onion (white and green parts), finely chopped

For the Peppers

- 8 ounces shishito peppers
- 1 tablespoon vegetable oil
- 1 teaspoon toasted sesame oil
- Kosher salt and black pepper
- ¼ to ½ teaspoon red pepper flakes (optional)
- ½ teaspoon toasted sesame seeds

CHERMOULA-ROASTED BEETS

Chermoula is a North African herb sauce, typically made with olive oil, cilantro, lemon juice, and garlic. Although it's traditionally served with meat or fish, I see no reason why veggies shouldn't get to enjoy its goodness as well. The rosy red beets along with the green-flecked sauce make for a great presentation. Go ahead and double up on the sauce so that you can use it with grilled meats or fish the next day.   **SERVINGS: 4**

PREP TIME: 15 MINUTES

COOK TIME: 25 MINUTES

ACTIVE TIME: 15 MINUTES

TOTAL TIME: 40 MINUTES

COOK TEMPERATURE: 375°F

1. **For the chermoula:** In a food processor, combine the cilantro, parsley, garlic, paprika, cumin, coriander, and cayenne. Pulse until coarsely chopped. Add the saffron, if using, and process until combined. With the food processor running, slowly add the olive oil in a steady stream; process until the sauce is uniform. Season to taste with salt.

2. **For the beets:** In a large bowl, drizzle the beets with ½ cup of the chermoula (see Note), or enough to coat. Arrange the beets in the air fryer basket. Set the air fryer to 375°F for 25 to minutes, or until the beets are tender.

3. Transfer the beets to a serving platter. Sprinkle with chopped cilantro and parsley and serve.

NOTE

★ This makes about ½ cup chermoula. Store leftovers in an airtight container in the refrigerator for up to 3 days. Serve with chicken, fish, or roasted vegetables.

For the Chermoula

- 1 cup packed fresh cilantro leaves
- ½ cup packed fresh parsley leaves
- 6 cloves garlic, peeled
- 2 teaspoons smoked paprika
- 2 teaspoons ground cumin
- 1 teaspoon ground coriander
- ½ to 1 teaspoon cayenne pepper
  Pinch crushed saffron (optional)
- ½ cup extra-virgin olive oil
  Kosher salt

For the Beets

- 3 medium beets, trimmed, peeled, and cut into 1-inch chunks
- 2 tablespoons chopped fresh cilantro
- 2 tablespoons chopped fresh parsley

CHILE-CHEESE CORNBREAD WITH CORN

NUT-FREE, SOY-FREE, VEGETARIAN

Double down on the corn, add some green chiles, and you've got a cornbread that's chewy, substantive, and just delightful. I used canned corn for this, but thawed frozen corn will work just as well. The green chiles are mild poblano chiles. Use a Bundt pan so that the center of the cornbread cooks quickly.   **SERVINGS: 6**

PREP TIME: 10 MINUTES

COOK TIME: 15 MINUTES

ACTIVE TIME: 10 MINUTES

STANDING TIME: 10 MINUTES

TOTAL TIME: 35 MINUTES

COOK TEMPERATURE: 350°F

1. In a medium bowl, whisk together the eggs and milk. Add the muffin mix and stir until the batter is smooth. Stir in the corn, cheese, and undrained chiles.

2. Spray a 3-cup Bundt pan with vegetable oil spray. Line the pan with parchment paper. (To do this, cut a circle of parchment about 1 inch larger in diameter than the top of the pan. Fold the parchment in half and cut a hole in the middle to accommodate the center of the Bundt pan. Place the parchment in the pan; trim any excess parchment from around the top.)

3. Pour the batter into the prepared pan. Place the pan in the air fryer basket. Set the air fryer to 350°F for 15 minutes.

4. Allow the bread to rest in the closed air fryer for 10 minutes before serving.

2   large eggs

¼   cup whole milk

1   (8.5-ounce) package corn muffin mix

1   cup corn kernels

½   cup grated cheddar cheese

1   (4-ounce) can diced mild green chiles, undrained

Vegetable oil spray

Parchment paper

VEGETABLES

CRISPY SESAME-GINGER BROCCOLI

GRAIN-FREE, GLUTEN-FREE,
EGG-FREE, NUT-FREE,
SOY-FREE, DAIRY-FREE,
VEGAN, LOW-CARB

I tried this with fresh broccoli. I tried it at a variety of temperatures. I had a house that smelled of burned broccoli! If you like broccoli, this recipe alone will be worth the price of this book. This is not just because it's easy and tasty, but because that burned broccoli smell in your house? Yeah, it lasts for days! But my testing has made this a nonissue for you. You're welcome. **SERVINGS: 4**

PREP TIME: 10 MINUTES

COOK TIME: 15 MINUTES

ACTIVE TIME: 10 MINUTES

TOTAL TIME: 25 MINUTES

COOK TEMPERATURE: 325°F

1. In a large bowl, combine the sesame oil, sesame seeds, chili-garlic sauce, ginger, salt, and pepper. Stir until well combined. Add the broccoli and toss until well coated.

2. Arrange the broccoli in the air fryer basket. Set the air fryer to 325°F for 15 minutes, or until the broccoli is crisp, tender, and the edges are lightly browned, gently tossing halfway through the cooking time.

3 tablespoons toasted sesame oil

2 teaspoons sesame seeds

1 tablespoon chili-garlic sauce

2 teaspoons minced fresh ginger

½ teaspoon kosher salt

½ teaspoon black pepper

1 (16-ounce) package frozen broccoli florets (do not thaw)

FRIED PLANTAINS

Plantains are not the same as bananas, but I will tell you a secret—I often use green bananas in this recipe. They're lower in carbs, easier to find, and equally delicious. If you wanted to make tostones, you'd basically undercook the plantain slices a bit, remove them, smash them up, and then recook in the air fryer at 400°F for another 4 to 5 minutes.   SERVINGS: 2

GRAIN-FREE, GLUTEN-FREE, EGG-FREE, NUT-FREE, SOY-FREE, DAIRY-FREE, VEGAN

PREP TIME: 10 MINUTES
COOK TIME: 8 MINUTES
ACTIVE TIME: 10 MINUTES
TOTAL TIME: 18 MINUTES
COOK TEMPERATURE: 400°F

- 2 ripe plantains, peeled and cut at a diagonal into ½-inch-thick pieces
- 3 tablespoons ghee, melted
- ¼ teaspoon kosher salt

1. In a medium bowl, toss the plantains with the ghee and salt.

2. Arrange the plantain pieces in the air fryer basket. Set the air fryer to 400°F for 8 minutes. The plantains are done when they are soft and tender on the inside, and have plenty of crisp, sweet, brown spots on the outside. (The riper the plantains, the faster they will cook.)

VARIATIONS

★ Spicy Plantains: Add ⅛ to ¼ teaspoon cayenne pepper.
★ Garlic-Chile Plantains: Add ¼ teaspoon each garlic powder, ground cumin, and ancho chile powder.
★ Smoky Plantains: Add ¼ teaspoon smoked paprika.
★ Cinnamon-Sugar Plantains: Omit the salt. Toss with ¼ teaspoon ground cinnamon and 1 teaspoon sugar.

GREEN BEANS & BACON

If you're from the South, let me tell you up front, these green beans are squeakers. The rest of the country can rejoice in the fact that they are crisp, not mushy, green beans. But I think we can all celebrate the fact that they are *easy* and delicious. Starting with frozen green beans guarantees an easy-to-whip-up recipe that requires almost no preplanning.   **SERVINGS: 4**

GRAIN-FREE, GLUTEN-FREE,
EGG-FREE, NUT-FREE,
SOY-FREE, DAIRY-FREE,
LOW-CARB

PREP TIME: 10 MINUTES
COOK TIME: 20 MINUTES
ACTIVE TIME: 10 MINUTES
STANDING TIME: 5 MINUTES
TOTAL TIME: 35 MINUTES
COOK TEMPERATURE: 375°F/400°F

1. In a 6×3-inch round heatproof pan, combine the frozen green beans, onion, bacon, and water. Toss to combine. Place the pan in the air fryer basket. Set the air fryer to 375°F for 15 minutes.

2. Raise the air fryer temperature to 400°F for 5 minutes. Season the beans with salt and pepper to taste and toss well.

3. Remove the pan from the air fryer basket and cover with foil. Let the beans rest for 5 minutes before serving.

- 3 cups frozen cut green beans (do not thaw)
- 1 medium onion, chopped
- 3 slices bacon, chopped
- ¼ cup water
  Kosher salt and black pepper

MEXICAN CORN IN A CUP (ELOTE EN VASO)

GLUTEN-FREE, NUT-FREE, SOY-FREE, VEGETARIAN

PREP TIME: 5 MINUTES
COOK TIME: 10 MINUTES
ACTIVE TIME: 5 MINUTES
TOTAL TIME: 15 MINUTES
COOK TEMPERATURE: 350°F

If you can't go get *elote en vaso* from a little food cart near where you live, then this homemade version is the next best thing—or dare we say an even better thing? The air fryer does a surprisingly good job of cooking frozen corn. If your air fryer basket has a grid at the bottom or very large holes, you may need to place the corn in a heatproof pan. Otherwise, pour it directly into the basket and cook away! **SERVINGS: 4**

1. Place the corn in the bottom of the air fryer basket and spray with vegetable oil spray. Set the air fryer to 350°F for 10 minutes.

2. Transfer the corn to a serving bowl. Add the butter and stir until melted. Add the sour cream, mayonnaise, cheese, lemon juice, and chili powder; stir until well combined. Serve immediately with green onion and cilantro (if using).

4   cups (32-ounce bag) frozen corn kernels (do not thaw)

Vegetable oil spray

2   tablespoons butter

¼   cup sour cream

¼   cup mayonnaise

¼   cup grated Parmesan cheese (or feta, cotija, or queso fresco)

2   tablespoons fresh lemon or lime juice

1   teaspoon chili powder

Chopped fresh green onion (optional)

Chopped fresh cilantro (optional)

49

VEGETABLES

CREAMED SPINACH

I love spinach but I have stopped buying fresh spinach because I always end up throwing it out. I have great intentions when I buy it, but then four days later I open the vegetable drawer—I'm sure you know how this goes. Frozen spinach is not only convenient, but it's a lot more compact, which makes it easier to cook in an air fryer.   **SERVINGS: 4**

GRAIN-FREE, GLUTEN-FREE, EGG-FREE, NUT-FREE, SOY-FREE, VEGETARIAN, LOW-CARB

PREP TIME: 10 MINUTES
COOK TIME: 15 MINUTES
ACTIVE TIME: 10 MINUTES
TOTAL TIME: 25 MINUTES
COOK TEMPERATURE: 350°F/400°F

1. Spray a 6 × 3-inch round heatproof pan with vegetable oil spray.

2. In a medium bowl, combine the spinach, onion, garlic, cream cheese, nutmeg, salt, and pepper. Transfer to the prepared pan.

3. Place the pan in the air fryer basket. Set the air fryer to 350°F for 10 minutes. Open and stir to thoroughly combine the cream cheese and spinach.

4. Sprinkle the Parmesan cheese on top. Set the air fryer to 400°F for 5 minutes, or until the cheese has melted and browned.

Vegetable oil spray

1   (10-ounce) package frozen spinach, thawed and squeezed dry

½   cup chopped onion

2   cloves garlic, minced

4   ounces cream cheese, diced

½   teaspoon ground nutmeg

1   teaspoon kosher salt

1   teaspoon black pepper

½   cup grated Parmesan cheese

MUSHROOMS WITH GOAT CHEESE

GRAIN-FREE, GLUTEN-FREE,
EGG-FREE, NUT-FREE,
SOY-FREE, VEGETARIAN,
LOW-CARB

This recipe looks so simple—and when it's done, I admit that it's not that inspired-looking. But the taste? That's where it's all at. The mushrooms have just a little bit of give to them, the goat cheese is all melty and creamy, and it all just works together. You can serve it as a great low-carb side dish, but it also does very well over well-buttered toast. Do not add salt; the goat cheese is salty enough to flavor it.   **SERVINGS: 4**

PREP TIME: 10 MINUTES

COOK TIME: 10 MINUTES

ACTIVE TIME: 10 MINUTES

TOTAL TIME: 20 MINUTES

COOK TEMPERATURE: 400°F

1. In a 6 × 3-inch round heatproof pan, combine the oil, mushrooms, garlic, dried thyme, and pepper. Stir in the goat cheese. Place the pan in the air fryer basket. Set the air fryer to 400°F for 10 minutes, stirring halfway through the cooking time.

2. Sprinkle with fresh thyme, if desired.

3 tablespoons vegetable oil

1 pound mixed mushrooms, trimmed and sliced

1 clove garlic, minced

¼ teaspoon dried thyme

½ teaspoon black pepper

4 ounces goat cheese, diced

2 teaspoons chopped fresh thyme leaves (optional)

VEGETABLES

PASTA WITH MASCARPONE MUSHROOMS

GRAIN-FREE, GLUTEN-FREE, EGG-FREE, NUT-FREE, SOY-FREE, VEGETARIAN, LOW-CARB

PREP TIME: 10 MINUTES
COOK TIME: 15 MINUTES
ACTIVE TIME: 10 MINUTES
TOTAL TIME: 25 MINUTES
COOK TEMPERATURE: 350°F

Yes, you do have to make the pasta separately, but the sauce is so hands-off that it practically cooks itself, so you will have bought yourself some extra time! The combination of earthy mushrooms with creamy pasta makes for a wonderful blend of flavors.   **SERVINGS: 4**

1. Spray a 7×3-inch round heatproof pan with vegetable oil spray.

2. In a medium bowl, combine the mushrooms, onion, garlic, cream, mascarpone, thyme, salt, black pepper, and red pepper flakes. Stir to combine. Transfer the mixture to the prepared pan.

3. Place the pan in the air fryer basket. Set the air fryer to 350°F for 15 minutes, stirring halfway through the cooking time.

4. Divide the pasta among four shallow bowls. Spoon the mushroom mixture evenly over the pasta. Sprinkle with Parmesan cheese and serve.

Vegetable oil spray

4 cups sliced mushrooms

1 medium yellow onion, chopped

2 cloves garlic, minced

¼ cup heavy whipping cream or half-and-half

8 ounces mascarpone cheese

1 teaspoon dried thyme

1 teaspoon kosher salt

1 teaspoon black pepper

½ teaspoon red pepper flakes

4 cups cooked konjac noodles, cauliflower rice, linguine, or spaghetti, for serving

½ cup grated Parmesan cheese

RADISHES O'BRIEN

Potatoes O'Brien is a classic side dish dating back to the early 1900s made from fried, diced potatoes, and red and green bell peppers. I used that dish as inspiration for this one. This radish version is a little different in texture—I leave the radishes a little crunchier. If you want them softer, just increase the cook time and spray them well as you continue to cook them. Be sure that all of the vegetables are diced about the same size so they cook evenly.   SERVINGS: 4

GRAIN-FREE, GLUTEN-FREE, EGG-FREE, NUT-FREE, SOY-FREE, DAIRY-FREE, PALEO, VEGAN, LOW-CARB

PREP TIME: 10 MINUTES
COOK TIME: 23 MINUTES
ACTIVE TIME: 10 MINUTES
TOTAL TIME: 33 MINUTES
COOK TEMPERATURE: 350°F/400°F

1. In a large bowl, combine the radishes, onion, bell pepper, garlic, salt, and pepper. Pour the melted oil over the vegetables and mix well to coat.

2. Scrape the vegetables into the air fryer basket. Set the air fryer to 350°F for 20 minutes. Increase the temperature to 400°F for 3 minutes to crisp up the edges of the vegetables. Serve hot.

2½ cups whole radishes, trimmed, each cut into 8 wedges

1 medium yellow or white onion, diced

1 small green bell pepper, stemmed, seeded, and diced

4 to 6 cloves garlic, thinly sliced

½ to 1 teaspoon kosher salt

½ to 1 teaspoon black pepper

2 tablespoons coconut oil, melted

RAS AL HANOUT—ROASTED CARROTS WITH HARISSA SOUR CREAM

This is a great way to use the ras al hanout as well as the harissa that you will have made for other recipes. Of course, if you don't have any (I mean, what are you waiting for?!), you can always use store-bought seasonings, or use this as a base recipe for roasting baby carrots and reach for whatever spice combination strikes your fancy.   **SERVINGS: 4**

1. **For the harissa sour cream:** In a small bowl, combine the sour cream and harissa. Whisk until well combined. Cover and chill until ready to serve.

2. **For the carrots:** Place the carrots in a large bowl and drizzle with the olive oil. Toss to coat. Sprinkle with the ras al hanout and salt. Toss again to evenly coat the carrots.

3. Arrange the carrots in the air fryer basket. Set the air fryer to 400°F for 12 minutes, or until the carrots are tender and lightly charred on the edges, tossing halfway through the cooking time.

4. Transfer the carrots to a serving platter. Drizzle with the lemon juice and harissa sour cream. Sprinkle with the parsley and pistachios, if using.

GRAIN-FREE, GLUTEN-FREE, EGG-FREE, NUT-FREE, SOY-FREE, VEGETARIAN

PREP TIME: 10 MINUTES
COOK TIME: 12 MINUTES
ACTIVE TIME: 10 MINUTES
TOTAL TIME: 22 MINUTES
COOK TEMPERATURE: 400°F

For the Harissa Sour Cream

½ cup sour cream

1 tablespoon Harissa (page 184)

For the Carrots

3 cups baby carrots, halved lengthwise

2 tablespoons extra-virgin olive oil

1 teaspoon Ras al Hanout (page 188)

½ teaspoon kosher salt

1 tablespoon fresh lemon juice

Chopped fresh parsley, for garnish (optional)

Chopped roasted pistachios, for garnish (optional)

VEGETABLES

ROASTED CAULIFLOWER WITH CILANTRO-JALAPEÑO SAUCE

GRAIN-FREE, GLUTEN-FREE, EGG-FREE, NUT-FREE, SOY-FREE, VEGETARIAN, LOW-CARB

PREP TIME: 15 MINUTES
COOK TIME: 20 MINUTES
ACTIVE TIME: 15 MINUTES
TOTAL TIME: 35 MINUTES
COOK TEMPERATURE: 400°F

If you like roasted cauliflower, you'll love the ease of roasting it in your air fryer. If you like cilantro and jalapeño, you will like this dressing with just about anything. Behold! I give you two recipes in one—and the two can be used in a variety of other ways too. How's that for delicious efficiency?   **SERVINGS: 4**

1. **For the cauliflower:** In a large bowl, combine the cauliflower, oil, cumin, coriander, and salt. Toss to coat.

2. Place the cauliflower in the air fryer basket. Set the air fryer to 400°F for 20 minutes, stirring halfway through the cooking time.

3. **Meanwhile, for the sauce:** In a blender, combine the yogurt, cilantro, jalapeño, garlic, and salt. Blend, adding the water as needed to keep the blades moving and to thin the sauce if needed.

4. At the end of cooking time, transfer the cauliflower to a large serving bowl. Pour the sauce over and toss gently to coat. Serve immediately.

For the Cauliflower

- 5 cups cauliflower florets (about 1 large head)
- 3 tablespoons vegetable oil
- ½ teaspoon ground cumin
- ½ teaspoon ground coriander
- ½ teaspoon kosher salt

For the Sauce

- ½ cup Greek yogurt or sour cream
- ¼ cup chopped fresh cilantro
- 1 jalapeño, seeded and coarsely chopped
- 4 cloves garlic, peeled
- ½ teaspoon kosher salt
- 2 tablespoons water

ROASTED RATATOUILLE

GRAIN-FREE, GLUTEN-FREE,
EGG-FREE, NUT-FREE,
SOY-FREE, DAIRY-FREE,
PALEO, VEGAN, LOW-CARB

I love ratatouille but I don't love the laborious arranging of it in concentric circles because I really don't have that kind of patience—nor the attention span, if truth be told. I also find the veggies to be a little less crisp in that process. So, I decided to use the ingredients of a ratatouille but roast them to get a delightfully savory and slightly crisp dish. The vegetables shrink down considerably after cooking. You will get about 2 cups of cooked veggies from this recipe, making it a great side dish.   **SERVINGS: 2 TO 3**

PREP TIME: 15 MINUTES

COOK TIME: 20 MINUTES

ACTIVE TIME: 15 MINUTES

TOTAL TIME: 35 MINUTES

COOK TEMPERATURE: 400°F

1. In a medium bowl, combine the eggplant, bell pepper, tomatoes, garlic, oil, oregano, thyme, salt, and pepper. Toss to combine.

2. Place the vegetables in the air fryer basket. Set the air fryer to 400°F for 20 minutes, or until the vegetables are crisp-tender.

2 cups ¾-inch cubed peeled eggplant

1 small red, yellow, or orange bell pepper, stemmed, seeded, and diced

1 cup cherry tomatoes

6 to 8 cloves garlic, peeled and halved lengthwise

3 tablespoons olive oil

1 teaspoon dried oregano

½ teaspoon dried thyme

1 teaspoon kosher salt

½ teaspoon black pepper

ROSEMARY & CHEESE–ROASTED RED POTATOES

GRAIN-FREE, GLUTEN-FREE, EGG-FREE, NUT-FREE, SOY-FREE, VEGETARIAN

Roasted potatoes are the star of any meal as far as I am concerned. But I like making them different ways. My rosemary bushes were out of control last spring, so I used some in this unusual but very tasty combination. You could use the same flavors to make roasted cauliflower as well.   **SERVINGS: 4**

PREP TIME: 10 MINUTES

COOK TIME: 15 MINUTES

ACTIVE TIME: 10 MINUTES

TOTAL TIME: 25 MINUTES

COOK TEMPERATURE: 400°F

1. In a large bowl, toss together the potatoes, olive oil, rosemary, garlic powder, salt and pepper to taste, and ¼ cup of the Parmesan until the potatoes are well coated.

2. Place the seasoned potatoes in the air fryer basket. Set the air fryer to 400°F for 15 minutes, or until potatoes are tender when pierced with a fork.

3. Transfer the potatoes to a serving platter or bowl. Toss with the remaining 1 tablespoon Parmesan and the parsley.

- 4 cups quartered baby red potatoes
- 3 tablespoons extra-virgin olive oil
- 2 teaspoons chopped fresh rosemary
- ¼ teaspoon garlic powder

  Kosher salt and black pepper
- ¼ cup plus 1 tablespoon finely grated Parmesan cheese
- ¼ cup chopped fresh parsley

SPICED BUTTERNUT SQUASH

GRAIN-FREE, GLUTEN-FREE,
EGG-FREE, NUT-FREE,
SOY-FREE, DAIRY-FREE,
VEGAN

I love the star anise flavor in five-spice powder, and combining that with butternut squash is just heavenly. It's familiar-but-different, and will go with just about any sort of air-fried meat as a side.   **SERVINGS: 4**

PREP TIME: 10 MINUTES

COOK TIME: 15 MINUTES

ACTIVE TIME: 10 MINUTES

TOTAL TIME: 25 MINUTES

COOK TEMPERATURE: 400°F

1. In a medium bowl, combine the squash, oil, sugar, and five-spice powder. Toss to coat.

2. Place the squash in the air fryer basket. Set the air fryer to 400°F for 15 minutes or until tender.

4	cups 1-inch-cubed butternut squash
2	tablespoons vegetable oil
1 to 2	tablespoons brown sugar
1	teaspoon Chinese five-spice powder

VARIATIONS

★ Use pumpkin pie or apple pie spice instead of the five-spice powder.
★ Use ½ teaspoon ground cumin plus ½ teaspoon ground coriander instead of the five-spice powder.

SPICED GLAZED CARROTS

GRAIN-FREE, GLUTEN-FREE,
EGG-FREE, NUT-FREE,
SOY-FREE, DAIRY-FREE,
VEGAN

Yet another dish where we start with frozen veggies and end up with a delicious side dish. The addition of cumin and cinnamon adds unexpected flair. (If you avoid sugar, I've also made this with 2 tablespoons Swerve quite successfully.) **SERVINGS: 4**

PREP TIME: 10 MINUTES

COOK TIME: 30 MINUTES

ACTIVE TIME: 10 MINUTES

TOTAL TIME: 40 MINUTES

COOK TEMPERATURE: 400°F

1. Spray a 6 × 4-inch round heatproof pan with vegetable oil spray.

2. In a medium bowl, combine the carrots, brown sugar, water, cumin, cinnamon, and salt. Toss to coat. Transfer to the prepared pan. Dot the carrots with the coconut oil, distributing it evenly across the pan. Cover the pan with foil.

3. Place the pan in the air fryer basket. Set the air fryer to 400°F for 10 minutes. Remove the foil and stir well. Place the uncovered pan back in the air fryer. Set the air fryer to 400°F for 20 minutes, or until the glaze is bubbling and the carrots are cooked through.

4. Garnish with parsley and serve.

Vegetable oil spray

4 cups frozen sliced carrots (do not thaw)

2 tablespoons brown sugar

2 tablespoons water

½ teaspoon ground cumin

½ teaspoon ground cinnamon

¼ teaspoon kosher salt

2 tablespoons coconut oil

Chopped fresh parsley, for garnish

SPINACH & CHEESE–STUFFED TOMATOES

SPINACH & CHEESE–STUFFED TOMATOES

GRAIN-FREE, GLUTEN-FREE, EGG-FREE, NUT-FREE, SOY-FREE, VEGETARIAN, LOW-CARB

PREP TIME: 20 MINUTES

COOK TIME: 15 MINUTES

ACTIVE TIME: 20 MINUTES

TOTAL TIME: 35 MINUTES

COOK TEMPERATURE: 350°F

Our friends John and Diane fought over these tomatoes at one of the typical weekend meals we host at our house. They come over to taste the recipes that John and I tested that week. Sometimes we have four desserts for lunch. That day, we had a few meat dishes and three stuffed tomatoes to divide among us four. Take my advice, make sure you have at least one delicious tomato per person. You may want to double up on this recipe if you intend to serve them as a main dish. Otherwise, one tomato per person makes a good side dish. I usually use frozen spinach for these just because I always have it on hand, but if you have fresh, just microwave or precook the spinach long enough for it to cook down, then proceed with the recipe as written. **SERVINGS: 2**

- 4 ripe beefsteak tomatoes
- ¾ teaspoon black pepper
- ½ teaspoon kosher salt
- 1 (10-ounce) package frozen chopped spinach, thawed and squeezed dry
- 1 (5.2-ounce) package garlic-and-herb Boursin cheese
- 3 tablespoons sour cream
- ½ cup finely grated Parmesan cheese

1. Cut the tops off the tomatoes. Using a small spoon, carefully remove and discard the pulp. Season the insides with ½ teaspoon of the black pepper and ¼ teaspoon of the salt. Invert the tomatoes onto paper towels and allow to drain while you make the filling.

2. Meanwhile, in a medium bowl, combine the spinach, Boursin cheese, sour cream, ¼ cup of the Parmesan, and the remaining ¼ teaspoon salt and ¼ teaspoon pepper. Stir until ingredients are well combined. Divide the filling among the tomatoes. Top with the remaining ¼ cup Parmesan.

3. Place the tomatoes in the air fryer basket. Set the air fryer to 350°F for 15 minutes, or until the filling is hot.

RUSSET & SWEET POTATO GRATIN

GRAIN-FREE, GLUTEN-FREE,
EGG-FREE, NUT-FREE,
SOY-FREE, VEGETARIAN

Let me be honest with you, this may not be the prettiest dish you've ever created in your air fryer, but it will be so tasty, and so easy, that no one will care. Use a mandoline to get thin potato slices that cook faster, and be sure to cover the pan with foil to keep the top of the gratin from overcooking before the middle is finished. **SERVINGS: 4**

PREP TIME: 15 MINUTES
COOK TIME: 45 MINUTES
ACTIVE TIME: 15 MINUTES
STANDING TIME: 5 MINUTES
TOTAL TIME: 1 HOUR 5 MINUTES
COOK TEMPERATURE: 350°F/400°F

1. Spray a 6×3-inch round heatproof pan with vegetable oil spray; set aside.

2. In a blender, combine the cream, onion, garlic, thyme, salt, and pepper. Blend until smooth.

3. In a large bowl, combine the sliced russet and sweet potatoes. Drizzle with the oil and toss to coat. Transfer the potatoes to the prepared pan. Pour the cream mixture over the top of the potatoes.

4. Cover the pan with foil and place in the air fryer basket. Set the air fryer to 350°F for 40 minutes, or until potatoes are nearly tender.

5. Uncover and sprinkle with Parmesan cheese. Set the air fryer to 400°F for 5 minutes, or until the potatoes are bubbly with a golden-brown crust.

6. Let stand for 5 minutes before serving.

Vegetable oil spray

1 cup heavy whipping cream

¼ cup roughly chopped onion

3 cloves garlic, peeled

1 teaspoon chopped fresh thyme leaves

½ teaspoon kosher salt

½ teaspoon black pepper

1 medium russet potato, peeled and very thinly sliced (about 1½ cups)

1 medium sweet potato, peeled and very thinly sliced (about 1½ cups)

1 tablespoon vegetable oil

¼ cup grated Parmesan cheese

SWEET POTATO FRIES WITH AJI CRIOLLO MAYO

GRAIN-FREE, GLUTEN-FREE, NUT-FREE, SOY-FREE, DAIRY-FREE, PALEO, VEGETARIAN

It seems to me the first thing people make in their air fryers are fries. My previous air fryer cookbook tells you how to make excellent fries. (Hint: It's all in the type of potatoes and how you cut them.) But the mayo here—seasoned with the flavors of the Ecuadorian green hot sauce called *aji criollo*—will steal your heart. You will want to use it everywhere you can!   **SERVINGS: 2**

PREP TIME: 10 MINUTES
COOK TIME: 20 MINUTES
ACTIVE TIME: 30 MINUTES
TOTAL TIME: 30 MINUTES
COOK TEMPERATURE: 400°F

1. **For the fries:** Cut the potato lengthwise into ¼-inch-thick slices. Lay each slice flat and cut lengthwise into fries about ¼ inch thick.

2. In a medium bowl, toss together the potatoes, olive oil, paprika, garlic powder, onion powder, salt, and pepper until well coated.

3. Place the fries in a single layer in the air fryer basket. (If they won't fit in a single layer, set a rack or trivet on top of the bottom layer of potatoes and place the rest of the potatoes on the rack, or cook in multiple batches.) Set the air fryer to 400°F for 20 minutes, shaking halfway through the cooking time, or until the fries are tender and lightly browned.

4. **Meanwhile, for the mayonnaise:** In a blender, combine the mayonnaise, lime juice, vinegar, cilantro, parsley, green onion, jalapeños, garlic, and salt. Blend until smooth.

5. Turn the fries out onto a serving platter. Serve immediately with the mayonnaise for dipping.

For the Fries

- 1 large sweet potato, peeled
- 2 tablespoons extra-virgin olive oil
- ½ teaspoon smoked paprika
- ½ teaspoon garlic powder
- ½ teaspoon onion powder
- ¼ teaspoon kosher salt
- ¼ teaspoon black pepper

For the Aji Criollo Mayonnaise

- ½ cup mayonnaise
- 2 tablespoons fresh lime juice
- 2 teaspoons cider vinegar
- ½ bunch fresh cilantro, roughly chopped
- ¼ bunch fresh parsley, roughly chopped
- 1 green onion (white and green parts), chopped
- 2 jalapeños, seeded and chopped
- 2 cloves garlic, minced
- ¼ teaspoon kosher salt

SWEET & CRISPY ROASTED PEARL ONIONS

GRAIN-FREE, GLUTEN-FREE, EGG-FREE, NUT-FREE, SOY-FREE, DAIRY-FREE, PALEO, VEGAN, LOW-CARB

Thick, syrupy balsamic makes these pearl onions shine—and also makes them a perfect companion for grilled meats. Got leftovers? I mash them up and mix with sour cream to make a tasty dip. Pro tip: Use frozen onions so that you don't have to blanch and peel the tiny little fresh pearl onions.   SERVINGS: 3

PREP TIME: 5 MINUTES

COOK TIME: 18 MINUTES

ACTIVE TIME: 5 MINUTES

TOTAL TIME: 23 MINUTES

COOK TEMPERATURE: 400°F

1. In a medium bowl, combine the onions, olive oil, vinegar, rosemary, salt, and pepper until well coated.

2. Transfer the onions to the air fryer basket. Set the air fryer to 400°F for 18 minutes, or until the onions are tender and lightly charred, stirring once or twice during the cooking time.

1 (14.5-ounce) package frozen pearl onions (do not thaw)

2 tablespoons extra-virgin olive oil

2 tablespoons balsamic vinegar

2 teaspoons finely chopped fresh rosemary

½ teaspoon kosher salt

¼ teaspoon black pepper

ZUCCHINI & TOMATO SALAD

Here's yet another use for my wonderfully fragrant Lebanese Seven-Spice Mix. You can make the Baked Kibbe on page 127 one day and use the rest of the spice for this entirely different dish. #RuthlessEfficiency at work for sure.   **SERVINGS: 2 TO 3**

1. **For the salad:** In a medium bowl, whisk together the oil, spice mix, and cumin if using. Add the zucchini and tomatoes and toss to combine.

2. Spray the air fryer basket with olive oil spray. Place the zucchini and tomatoes in the air fryer basket. Set the air fryer to 400°F for 10 minutes. Transfer the vegetables to a serving bowl and let cool.

3. **Meanwhile, for the dressing:** In a small jar with a lid, combine all the ingredients and shake vigorously to combine.

4. Pour the dressing over the cooled vegetables, toss until well coated, and serve.

GRAIN-FREE, GLUTEN-FREE, EGG-FREE, NUT-FREE, SOY-FREE, DAIRY-FREE, PALEO, VEGAN, LOW-CARB

PREP TIME: 10 MINUTES
COOK TIME: 10 MINUTES
ACTIVE TIME: 10 MINUTES
TOTAL TIME: 20 MINUTES
COOK TEMPERATURE: 400°F

VEGETABLES

For the Salad

- 3 tablespoons olive oil
- 2 teaspoons Lebanese Seven-Spice Mix (page 186)
- ½ teaspoon ground cumin (optional)
- 1 medium zucchini, halved lengthwise and cut into chunks (about 2 cups)
- 1 cup cherry tomatoes
- Olive oil spray

For the Dressing

- ¼ cup olive oil
- 2 tablespoons fresh lemon juice
- ¼ cup chopped fresh parsley
- 2 tablespoons chopped fresh mint
- ½ to 1 teaspoon Lebanese Seven-Spice Mix
- ½ teaspoon kosher salt

CHICK
PO

EN/
ULTRY

BRAZILIAN TEMPERO BAIANO CHICKEN DRUMSTICKS

You're going to be so happy when you make these drumsticks! Your whole kitchen is going to smell fantastic, and everyone is going to think you're a great chef (which, let's face it, you are when you make food like this). Only you will know how easy it was to make. The savory tempero baiano spice blend, from the northern state of Bahia in Brazil, is also great for all sorts of grilled meats and vegetables. **SERVINGS: 4**

PREP TIME: 5 MINUTES
MARINATING TIME: 30 MINUTES
COOK TIME: 20 MINUTES
ACTIVE TIME: 5 MINUTES
TOTAL TIME: 55 MINUTES
COOK TEMPERATURE: 400°F

1. In a clean coffee grinder or spice mill, combine the cumin, oregano, parsley, turmeric, coriander seeds, salt, peppercorns, and cayenne. Process until finely ground.

2. In a small bowl, combine the ground spices with the lime juice and oil. Place the chicken in a resealable plastic bag. Add the marinade, seal, and massage until the chicken is well coated. Marinate at room temperature for 30 minutes or in the refrigerator for up to 24 hours.

3. When you are ready to cook, place the drumsticks skin side up in the air fryer basket. Set the air fryer to 400°F for 20 to 25 minutes, turning the legs halfway through the cooking time. Use a meat thermometer to ensure that the chicken has reached an internal temperature of 165°F.

4. Serve with plenty of napkins.

- 1 teaspoon cumin seeds
- 1 teaspoon dried oregano
- 1 teaspoon dried parsley
- 1 teaspoon ground turmeric
- ½ teaspoon coriander seeds
- 1 teaspoon kosher salt
- ½ teaspoon black peppercorns
- ½ teaspoon cayenne pepper
- ¼ cup fresh lime juice
- 2 tablespoons olive oil
- 1 ½ pounds chicken drumsticks

CHICKEN JALFREZI

The Indian curry called chicken jalfrezi (or jhalfrezi) is basically a fancy way of saying a chicken dish with stir-fried veggies. *Jhal* in Bengali means "spicy," so you can make this spicy. But essentially it's chicken, onion, and bell peppers coated in spices and served with a well-spiced tomato sauce. Doesn't that just sound delicious? **SERVINGS: 4**

GRAIN-FREE, GLUTEN-FREE, EGG-FREE, NUT-FREE, SOY-FREE, DAIRY-FREE, PALEO, LOW-CARB

PREP TIME: 15 MINUTES
COOK TIME: 15 MINUTES
ACTIVE TIME: 20 MINUTES
TOTAL TIME: 35 MINUTES
COOKING TEMPERATURE: 350°F

1. **For the chicken:** In a large bowl, combine the chicken, onion, bell pepper, oil, turmeric, garam masala, salt, and cayenne. Stir and toss until well combined.

2. Place the chicken and vegetables in the air fryer basket. Set the air fryer to 350°F for 15 minutes, stirring and tossing halfway through the cooking time. Use a meat thermometer to ensure the chicken has reached an internal temperature of 165°F.

3. **Meanwhile, for the sauce:** In a small microwave-safe bowl, combine the tomato sauce, water, garam masala, salt, and cayenne. Microwave on high for 1 minute. Remove and stir. Microwave for another minute; set aside.

4. When the chicken is cooked, remove and place chicken and vegetables in a large bowl. Pour the sauce over all. Stir and toss to coat the chicken and vegetables evenly.

5. Serve with rice, naan, or a side salad.

For the Chicken

- 1 pound boneless, skinless chicken thighs, cut into 2 or 3 pieces each
- 1 medium onion, chopped
- 1 large green bell pepper, stemmed, seeded, and chopped
- 2 tablespoons olive oil
- 1 teaspoon ground turmeric
- 1 teaspoon Garam Masala (page 183)
- 1 teaspoon kosher salt
- ½ to 1 teaspoon cayenne pepper

For the Sauce

- ¼ cup tomato sauce
- 1 tablespoon water
- 1 teaspoon Garam Masala (page 183)
- ½ teaspoon kosher salt
- ½ teaspoon cayenne pepper

  Side salad, rice, or naan bread, for serving

CHICKEN/POULTRY

CILANTRO CHICKEN KEBABS (HARIYALI KEBAB)

Hariyali means "green," and the cilantro sauce adds a wonderful tinge of fresh green herbs to this recipe. You really don't need to use skewers in an air fryer to make kebabs. Not only do the skewers take up room, but they don't really help cook the chicken any faster. If you really want to make the chicken look like kebabs, feel free to skewer the pieces after they're done cooking, if you can wait that long to eat them! **SERVINGS: 4**

1. **For the chutney:** In a blender or food processor, combine the coconut and hot water; set aside to soak for 5 minutes.

2. To the processor, add the cilantro, mint, garlic, and jalapeño, along with ¼ cup water. Blend at low speed, stopping occasionally to scrape down the sides. Add the lemon juice. With the blender or processor running, add only enough additional water to keep the contents moving. Turn the blender to high once the contents are moving freely and blend until the mixture is puréed.

3. **For the chicken:** Place the chicken pieces in a large bowl. Add ¼ cup of the chutney and mix well to coat. Set aside the remaining chutney to use as a dip. Marinate the chicken for 15 minutes at room temperature.

4. Spray the air fryer basket with olive oil spray. Arrange the chicken in the air fryer basket. Set the air fryer to 350°F for 10 minutes. Use a meat thermometer to ensure that the chicken has reached an internal temperature of 165°F.

5. Serve the chicken with the remaining chutney.

GRAIN-FREE, GLUTEN-FREE, EGG-FREE, NUT-FREE, SOY-FREE, DAIRY-FREE, PALEO, LOW-CARB

PREP TIME: 20 MINUTES
MARINATING TIME: 15 MINUTES
COOK TIME: 10 MINUTES
ACTIVE TIME: 20 MINUTES
TOTAL TIME: 45 MINUTES
COOK TEMPERATURE: 350°F

For the Chutney

- ½ cup unsweetened shredded coconut
- ½ cup hot water
- 2 cups fresh cilantro leaves, roughly chopped
- ¼ cup fresh mint leaves, roughly chopped
- 6 cloves garlic, roughly chopped
- 1 jalapeño, seeded and roughly chopped
- ¼ to ¾ cup water, as needed
- Juice of 1 lemon

For the Chicken

- 1 pound boneless, skinless chicken thighs, cut crosswise into thirds
- Olive oil spray

NOTE

★ *Kecap manis* is a dark brown, syrup-like sauce made from soybeans. It is similar to soy sauce, but has a sweeter, more complex flavor, as it is sweetened with palm sugar and usually seasoned with garlic and star anise.

★ To make your own kecap manis: In a small saucepan, combine 1 cup soy sauce; 1¼ cups palm sugar; 3 cloves garlic, halved; 2-inch piece fresh ginger, peeled and quartered; 2 star anise; and 2 whole cloves. Bring to a boil over medium heat, stirring occasionally. Reduce to low and simmer, stirring frequently, until the sauce begins to thicken, 10 to 15 minutes. Remove from heat and let cool completely (the sauce will continue to thicken as it cools). Strain the sauce and discard the spices and garlic. Makes 1 cup. Store in an airtight container in the refrigerator for up to 1 week.

CRISPY INDONESIAN CHICKEN WINGS

PREP TIME: 10 MINUTES
COOK TIME: 25 MINUTES
ACTIVE TIME: 15 MINUTES
TOTAL TIME: 40 MINUTES
COOK TEMPERATURE: 400°F

The wonderfully sweet and spicy combination of kecap manis and sambal is a shortcut to the traditional Indonesian sambal kecap. These chicken wings are so perfect for the air fryer. They cook quickly, and all the fat collects at the bottom of the pan, allowing the skin to get super crispy.   **SERVINGS: 2 TO 3**

1. **For the chicken:** In a large bowl, drizzle the chicken with the oil, sprinkle with the salt and pepper, and toss to coat.

2. Place the wings in the air fryer basket. Set the air fryer to 400°F for 20 minutes, turning once halfway through the cooking time.

3. **Meanwhile, for the sauce:** In a small bowl stir together the kecap manis, sambal oelek, and Worcestershire sauce.

4. Transfer the wings to a clean, large bowl. Drizzle with about half of the sauce and toss to coat. Return the wings to the air fryer. Set the air fryer to 400°F for 5 minutes more, or until the wings' skin is browned and crisp.

5. Return the wings the bowl and drizzle with the remaining sauce. Toss to coat. Transfer the wings to a serving platter and sprinkle with cilantro.

For the Chicken

- 1   pound chicken wings
- 1   tablespoon vegetable oil
- ½   teaspoon kosher salt
- ¼   teaspoon black pepper

For the Sauce

- ¼   cup kecap manis (see Note)
- 2   tablespoons sambal oelek chile sauce
- 2   tablespoons Worcestershire sauce

   Chopped fresh cilantro, for garnish

CURRY MUSTARD CHICKEN

There's a certain fast food restaurant that does these chicken tenders; this is my easy, delicious version. It's one of the few instances where I condone the use of ready-made curry powder.   **SERVINGS: 4**

1. In a large bowl, whisk together the mayonnaise, mustard, honey (if using), curry powder, salt, and cayenne. Transfer half of the mixture to a serving bowl to serve as a dipping sauce. Add the chicken tenders to the large bowl and toss and stir until well coated.

2. Place the tenders in the air fryer basket. Set the air fryer to 350°F for 15 minutes. Use a meat thermometer to ensure the chicken has reached an internal temperature of 165°F.

3. Serve the chicken with the dipping sauce.

GRAIN-FREE, GLUTEN-FREE, NUT-FREE, SOY-FREE, DAIRY-FREE, PALEO, LOW-CARB

PREP TIME: 10 MINUTES
COOK TIME: 15 MINUTES
ACTIVE TIME: 10 MINUTES
TOTAL TIME: 25 MINUTES
COOK TEMPERATURE: 350°F

- 6 tablespoons mayonnaise
- 2 tablespoons coarse-ground mustard
- 2 teaspoons honey (optional)
- 2 teaspoons curry powder
- 1 teaspoon kosher salt
- 1 teaspoon cayenne pepper
- 1 pound chicken tenders

FRENCH GARLIC CHICKEN

GRAIN-FREE, GLUTEN-FREE, EGG-FREE, NUT-FREE, SOY-FREE, LOW-CARB

PREP TIME: 10 MINUTES
MARINATING TIME: 30 MINUTES
COOK TIME: 27 MINUTES
ACTIVE TIME: 15 MINUTES
TOTAL TIME: 1 HOUR 15 MINUTES
COOK TEMPERATURE: 400°F/350°F

This is one of my most popular Instant Pot recipes, but I found that cooking it in the air fryer enhances the garlicky flavor, making it a lovely dish for company, or just for a quick family meal. Even the mustard-haters in my TwoSleevers groups seem to love the creamy, tangy sauce.   **SERVINGS: 4**

1. In a small bowl, combine the olive oil, mustard, vinegar, minced garlic, herbes de Provence, salt, and pepper. Use a wire whisk to emulsify the mixture.

2. Pierce the chicken all over with a fork to allow the marinade to penetrate better. Place the chicken in a resealable plastic bag, pour the marinade over, and seal. Massage until the chicken is well coated. Marinate at room temperature for 30 minutes or in the refrigerator for up to 24 hours.

3. When you are ready to cook, place the butter and chopped garlic in a 7 × 3-inch round heatproof pan and place it in the air fryer basket. Set the air fryer to 400°F for 5 minutes, or until the butter has melted and the garlic is sizzling.

4. Add the chicken and the marinade to the seasoned butter. Set the air fryer to 350°F for 15 minutes. Use a meat thermometer to ensure the chicken has reached an internal temperature of 165°F. Transfer the chicken to a plate and cover lightly with foil to keep warm.

5. Add the cream to the pan, stirring to combine with the garlic, butter, and cooking juices. Place the pan in the air fryer basket. Set the air fryer to 350°F for 7 minutes.

6. Pour the thickened sauce over the chicken and serve.

2 tablespoon extra-virgin olive oil

1 tablespoon Dijon mustard

1 tablespoon apple cider vinegar

3 cloves garlic, minced

2 teaspoons herbes de Provence

½ teaspoon kosher salt

1 teaspoon black pepper

1 pound boneless, skinless chicken thighs, halved crosswise

2 tablespoons butter

8 cloves garlic, chopped

¼ cup heavy whipping cream

LEBANESE TURKEY BURGERS WITH FETA & TZATZIKI

GRAIN-FREE, GLUTEN-FREE, EGG-FREE, NUT-FREE, SOY-FREE, LOW-CARB

This is just one of the many ways you can use my delicious Lebanese spice mix. Burgers in the air fryer are easy, fast, and delicious. They do shrink quite a bit, so it is okay to crowd them into the basket. I sometimes form the ground meat mixture into meatballs and serve them just with the sauce for a grain-free dinner. **SERVINGS: 4**

PREP TIME: 25 MINUTES
COOK TIME: 12 MINUTES
ACTIVE TIME: 25 MINUTES
TOTAL TIME: 37 MINUTES
COOK TEMPERATURE: 400°F

1. **For the tzatziki:** In a medium bowl, stir together all the ingredients until well combined. Cover and chill until ready to serve.

2. **For the burgers:** In a large bowl, combine the ground turkey, onion, garlic, parsley, spice mix, and salt. Mix gently until well combined. Divide the turkey into four portions and form into round patties.

3. Spray the air fryer basket with vegetable oil spray. Place the patties in a single layer in the air fryer basket. Set the air fryer to 400°F for 12 minutes. Use a meat thermometer to ensure the burgers have reached an internal temperature of 165°F (for turkey or chicken) or 160°F (for lamb).

4. Place one burger in each lettuce leaf or pita half. Tuck in 2 tomato slices, spinach, cheese, and some tzatziki.

NOTE

★ This makes about 3 cups tzatziki. Store leftovers in an airtight container in the refrigerator for up to 1 day.

For the Tzatziki

- 1   large cucumber, peeled and grated (about 2 cups)
- 2   to 3 cloves garlic, minced
- 1   cup plain Greek yogurt
- 1   tablespoon tahini (sesame paste)
- 1   tablespoon fresh lemon juice
- ½   teaspoon kosher salt

For the Burgers

- 1   pound ground turkey, chicken, or lamb
- 1   small yellow onion, finely diced
- 1   clove garlic, minced
- 2   tablespoons chopped fresh parsley
- 2   teaspoons Lebanese Seven-Spice Mix (page 186)
- ½   teaspoon kosher salt
      Vegetable oil spray

For Serving

- 4   lettuce leaves or 2 whole-wheat pita breads, halved
- 8   slices ripe tomato
- 1   cup baby spinach
- ⅓   cup crumbled feta cheese

ONE-DISH CHICKEN & RICE

I love dishes that give you an entire dinner in one shot. I was very curious as to whether you could make rice in the air fryer. Technically, it shouldn't be an issue, but it took a little experimenting with times, water quantities, etc. And now you have an easy supper to get on the table. Feel free to experiment with making the rice with a variety of flavorings now that you have this base recipe to play with. **SERVINGS: 4**

GLUTEN-FREE, EGG-FREE, NUT-FREE, SOY-FREE, DAIRY-FREE

PREP TIME: 10 MINUTES
COOK TIME: 40 MINUTES
ACTIVE TIME: 10 MINUTES
TOTAL TIME: 50 MINUTES
COOK TEMPERATURE: 375°F/400°F

1 cup long-grain white rice, rinsed and drained

1 cup cut frozen green beans (do not thaw)

1 tablespoon minced fresh ginger

3 cloves garlic, minced

1 tablespoon toasted sesame oil

1 teaspoon kosher salt

1 teaspoon black pepper

1 pound chicken wings, preferably drumettes

1. In a 6 × 3-inch round heatproof pan, combine the rice, green beans, ginger, garlic, sesame oil, salt, and pepper. Stir to combine. Place the chicken wings on top of the rice mixture.

2. Cover the pan with foil. Make a long slash in the foil to allow the pan to vent steam. Place the pan in the air fryer basket. Set the air fryer to 375°F for 30 minutes.

3. Remove the foil. Set the air fryer to 400°F for 10 minutes, or until the wings have browned and rendered fat into the rice and vegetables, turning the wings halfway through the cooking time.

PEANUT CHICKEN

Here's another use for the sweet chili sauce you bought for the Bang Shrimp on page 105. Peanut chicken is reminiscent of chicken satay, but with a lot less work. Pair it with a salad for a low-carb supper or with steamed rice for a great dinner. Speaking of less work, feel free to double the sauce Ingredients and save half in the refrigerator for up to a week. Use it to marinate your favorite meat and vegetables, then air fry and dinner is ready.   **SERVINGS: 4**

PREP TIME: 15 MINUTES
MARINATING TIME: 30 MINUTES
COOK TIME: 20 MINUTES
ACTIVE TIME: 15 MINUTES
TOTAL TIME: 1 HOUR 5 MINUTES
COOK TEMPERATURE: 350°F

1. In a small bowl, combine the peanut butter, sweet chili sauce, lime juice, sriracha, soy sauce, ginger, garlic, and salt. Add the hot water and whisk until smooth.

2. Place the chicken in a resealable plastic bag and pour in half of the sauce. (Reserve the remaining sauce for serving.) Seal the bag and massage until all of the chicken is well coated. Marinate at room temperature for 30 minutes or in the refrigerator for up to 24 hours.

3. Remove the chicken from the bag and discard the marinade. Place the chicken in the air fryer basket. Set the air fryer to 350°F for 20 minutes. Use a meat thermometer to ensure the chicken has reached an internal temperature of 165°F.

4. Transfer the chicken to a serving platter. Sprinkle with the cilantro, green onions, and peanuts. Serve with the reserved sauce for dipping.

NOTE

★ I use Mae Ploy Asian-inspired sweet chili marinade in this recipe, but you can use any sweet chili sauce.

- ¼ cup creamy peanut butter
- 2 tablespoons sweet chili sauce (see Note)
- 2 tablespoons fresh lime juice
- 1 tablespoon sriracha
- 1 tablespoon soy sauce
- 1 teaspoon minced fresh ginger
- 1 clove garlic, minced
- ½ teaspoon kosher salt
- ½ cup hot water
- 1 pound bone-in chicken thighs
- 2 tablespoons chopped fresh cilantro, for garnish
- ¼ cup chopped green onions, for garnish
- 2 to 3 tablespoons crushed roasted and salted peanuts, for garnish

SOUTH INDIAN PEPPER CHICKEN

GRAIN-FREE, GLUTEN-FREE,
EGG-FREE, NUT-FREE,
SOY-FREE, DAIRY-FREE,
PALEO, LOW-CARB

There isn't really a dish quite like this in South India, but the combination of flavors—fennel, cinnamon, black pepper, and cardamom— is quintessentially South Indian. **SERVINGS: 4**

PREP TIME: 20 MINUTES
MARINATING TIME: 30 MINUTES
COOK TIME: 15 MINUTES
ACTIVE TIME: 20 MINUTES
TOTAL TIME: 1 HOUR 5 MINUTES
COOK TEMPERATURE: 350°F/400°F

1. **For the spice mix:** Combine the dried chile, cinnamon, coriander, fennel, cumin, peppercorns, and cardamom in a clean coffee or spice grinder. Grind, shaking the grinder lightly so all the seeds and bits get into the blades, until the mixture is broken down to a fine powder. Stir in the turmeric and salt.

2. **For the chicken:** Place the chicken and onions in resealable plastic bag. Add the oil and 1½ tablespoons of the spice mix. Seal the bag and massage until the chicken is well coated. Marinate at room temperature for 30 minutes or in the refrigerator for up to 24 hours.

3. Place the chicken and onions in the air fryer basket. Set the air fryer to 350°F for 10 minutes, stirring once halfway through the cooking time. Increase the temperature to 400°F for 5 minutes. Use a meat thermometer to ensure the chicken has reached an internal temperature of 165°F.

4. Serve with steamed rice, cauliflower rice, or naan.

NOTE

★ This recipe makes 3 tablespoons spice mix. Store the remaining spice mix in an airtight container in a cool, dark place for up to 3 months.

For the Spice Mix

- 1   dried red chile, or
  ½ teaspoon dried red pepper flakes

  1-inch piece cinnamon or cassia bark
- 1½   teaspoons coriander seeds
- 1   teaspoon fennel seeds
- 1   teaspoon cumin seeds
- 1   teaspoon black peppercorns
- ½   teaspoon cardamom seeds
- ¼   teaspoon ground turmeric
- 1   teaspoon kosher salt

For the Chicken

- 1   pound boneless, skinless chicken thighs, cut crosswise into thirds
- 2   medium onions, cut into ½-inch-thick slices
- ¼   cup olive oil

  Cauliflower rice, steamed rice, or naan bread, for serving

PESTO-CREAM CHICKEN WITH CHERRY TOMATOES

GRAIN-FREE, GLUTEN-FREE, EGG-FREE, SOY-FREE, LOW-CARB

Sure, you could make your own pesto for this recipe—but if you're in a hurry, buy some good-quality pesto and make the lovely, herby, creamy sauce to go along with your chicken and enjoy. The chicken is also great as leftovers.   **SERVINGS: 4**

PREP TIME: 10 MINUTES
COOK TIME: 15 MINUTES
ACTIVE TIME: 10 MINUTES
TOTAL TIME: 25 MINUTES
COOK TEMPERATURE: 350°F

1. Spray a 6 × 3-inch round heatproof pan with vegetable oil spray; set aside.

2. In a large bowl, combine the pesto, half-and-half, cheese, and red pepper flakes. Whisk until well combined. Add the chicken and turn to coat.

3. Transfer the sauce and chicken to the prepared pan. Scatter the onion, bell pepper, and tomatoes on top. Place the pan in the air fryer basket. Set the air fryer to 350°F for 15 minutes. Use a meat thermometer to ensure the chicken has reached an internal temperature of 165°F.

Vegetable oil spray

½ cup prepared pesto

¼ cup half-and-half

¼ grated Parmesan cheese

½ to 1 teaspoon red pepper flakes

1 pound boneless, skinless chicken thighs, halved crosswise

1 small onion, sliced

½ cup sliced red and/or green bell peppers

½ cup halved cherry tomatoes

SPICY ROAST CHICKEN

Don't omit the vinegar here as it really adds a piquancy that makes this chicken just that little bit different from your usual chicken dishes. You could easily double the recipe and have delicious leftovers on hand for another day. **SERVINGS: 4**

1. In a small bowl, combine the turmeric, cayenne, cinnamon, cloves, salt, vinegar, and oil. Stir to form a thick paste.

2. Place the chicken in a resealable plastic bag and add the marinade. Seal the bag and massage until the chicken is well coated. Marinate at room temperature for 30 minutes or in the refrigerator for up to 24 hours.

3. Place the chicken in the air fryer basket. Set the air fryer to 350°F for 10 minutes, turning the chicken halfway through the cooking time. Use a meat thermometer to ensure that the chicken has reached an internal temperature of 165°F.

4. Serve with steamed rice or naan, over zoodles, or with a mixed salad.

GRAIN-FREE, GLUTEN-FREE, EGG-FREE, NUT-FREE, SOY-FREE, DAIRY-FREE, PALEO, LOW-CARB

PREP TIME: 10 MINUTES
MARINATING TIME: 30 MINUTES
COOK TIME: 10 MINUTES
ACTIVE TIME: 10 MINUTES
TOTAL TIME: 50 MINUTES
COOK TEMPERATURE: 350°F

1	teaspoon ground turmeric
½	teaspoon cayenne pepper
½	teaspoon ground cinnamon
¼	teaspoon ground cloves
¼	teaspoon kosher salt
1	tablespoon cider vinegar
2	tablespoons olive oil
1	pound boneless, skinless chicken thighs, cut crosswise into thirds
	Zoodles, steamed rice, naan bread, or a mixed salad, for serving

SEAF

OOD

BANG BANG SHRIMP

Sweet, spicy, savory, and easy? Yup, sign me up! It's all about the sauce in this recipe, but even that comes together quickly. I opted to skip the traditional breading for the shrimp so we could focus on the saucy goodness.   **SERVINGS: 4**

GLUTEN-FREE, NUT-FREE,
SOY-FREE, DAIRY-FREE

PREP TIME: 15 MINUTES
COOK TIME: 14 MINUTES
ACTIVE TIME: 15 MINUTES
TOTAL TIME: 30 MINUTES
COOK TEMPERATURE: 350°F

1. **For the sauce:** In a large bowl, combine the mayonnaise, chili sauce, sriracha, and ginger. Stir until well combined. Remove half of the sauce to serve as a dipping sauce.

2. **For the shrimp:** Place the shrimp in a medium bowl. Sprinkle the cornstarch and salt over the shrimp and toss until well coated.

3. Place the shrimp in the air fryer basket in a single layer. (If they won't fit in a single layer, set a rack or trivet on top of the bottom layer of shrimp and place the rest of the shrimp on the rack.) Spray generously with vegetable oil spray. Set the air fryer to 350°F for 10 minutes, turning and spraying with additional oil spray halfway through the cooking time.

4. Remove the shrimp and toss in the bowl with half of the sauce. Place the shrimp back in the air fryer basket. Set the air fryer to 350°F for an additional 4 to 5 minutes, or until the sauce has formed a glaze.

5. Serve the hot shrimp with the reserved sauce for dipping.

For the Sauce

- ½ cup mayonnaise
- ¼ cup sweet chili sauce
- 2 to 4 tablespoons sriracha
- 1 teaspoon minced fresh ginger

For the Shrimp

- 1 pound jumbo raw shrimp (21 to 25 count), peeled and deveined
- 2 tablespoons cornstarch or rice flour
- ½ teaspoon kosher salt

    Vegetable oil spray

CAJUN FRIED SHRIMP WITH REMOULADE

If you're dying for some fried shrimp out of your air fryer, here's the recipe for you. I make extra remoulade and use it with everything, including burgers, the next day.   **SERVINGS: 4**

1. **For the remoulade:** In a small bowl, stir together all the ingredients until well combined. Cover the sauce and chill until serving time.

2. **For the shrimp:** In a large bowl, whisk together the buttermilk, egg, and 1 teaspoon of the Cajun seasoning. Add the shrimp and toss gently to combine. Refrigerate for at least 15 minutes, or up to 1 hour.

3. Meanwhile, in a shallow dish, whisk together the remaining 2 teaspoons Cajun seasoning, cornmeal, and salt and pepper to taste.

4. Spray the air fryer basket with the vegetable oil spray. Dredge the shrimp in the cornmeal mixture until well coated. Shake off any excess and arrange the shrimp in the air fryer basket. Spray with oil spray.

5. Set the air fryer to 350°F for 8 minutes, carefully turning and spraying the shrimp with the oil spray halfway through the cooking time.

6. Serve the shrimp with the remoulade.

GLUTEN-FREE, NUT-FREE, SOY-FREE, LOW-CARB

PREP TIME: 30 MINUTES
CHILL TIME: 15 MINUTES
COOK TIME: 8 MINUTES
ACTIVE TIME: 30 MINUTES
TOTAL TIME: 53 MINUTES
COOK TEMPERATURE: 350°F

For the Remoulade

- ½ cup mayonnaise
- 1 green onion, finely chopped
- 1 clove garlic, minced
- 1 tablespoon sweet pickle relish
- 2 tablespoons Creole mustard
- 2 teaspoons fresh lemon juice
- ½ teaspoon hot pepper sauce
- ½ teaspoon Worcestershire sauce
- ¼ teaspoon smoked paprika
- ¼ teaspoon kosher salt

For the Shrimp

- 1½ cups buttermilk
- 1 large egg
- 3 teaspoons salt-free Cajun seasoning (page 182)
- 1 pound jumbo raw shrimp (21 to 25 count), peeled and deveined
- 2 cups finely ground cornmeal
- Kosher salt and black pepper
- Vegetable oil spray

GARLIC PEANUT SHRIMP

This is one of those recipes that happen when something you're trying to make fails, but it tastes so good you keep it anyway. I was trying to coat shrimp with the peanut mixture. Yeah, not so much. I did however get a very delicious savory peanut mix that nestles alongside the shrimp to yield a very tasty combination! I would serve this either by itself or with a salad. You could also try it mixed with sticky rice. If you can't find Spanish peanuts, just use regular roasted peanuts.   **SERVINGS: 4**

GRAIN-FREE, GLUTEN-FREE, EGG-FREE, SOY-FREE, DAIRY-FREE, LOW-CARB

PREP TIME: 15 MINUTES
COOK TIME: 10 MINUTES
ACTIVE TIME: 15 MINUTES
STANDING TIME: 5 MINUTES
TOTAL TIME: 30 MINUTES
COOK TEMPERATURE: 400°F/350°F

1. **For the peanut mix:** In a 6 × 3-inch round heatproof pan, combine all the ingredients and toss. Place the pan in the air fryer basket. Set the air fryer to 400°F for 5 minutes, or until all the spices are toasted. Remove the pan from the air fryer and let the mixture cool.

2. When completely cool, transfer the mixture to a mortar and pestle or clean coffee or spice grinder; crush or pulse to a very coarse texture that won't fall through the grate of the air fryer basket.

3. **For the shrimp:** In a large bowl, combine the shrimp and oil. Toss until well combined. Add the peanut mix and toss again. Place the shrimp and peanut mix in the air fryer basket. Set the air fryer to 350°F for 5 minutes.

4. Transfer to a serving dish. Cover and allow the shrimp to finish cooking in the residual heat, about 5 minutes. Serve with lime wedges.

For the Peanut Mix

- 1 cup roasted and salted red-skinned Spanish peanuts
- 8 cloves garlic, smashed and peeled
- 3 dried red arbol chiles, broken into pieces
- 1 tablespoon cumin seeds
- 2 teaspoons vegetable oil

For the Shrimp

- 1 pound jumbo raw shrimp (21 to 25 count), peeled and deveined
- 2 tablespoons vegetable oil
  Lime wedges, for serving

GREEN CURRY SHRIMP

Before you write to me, angrily telling me that half-and-half doesn't belong in a Thai dish, let me defend myself. Look, I'm not the type of person that opens up a 14-ounce can of coconut milk so I can use 1 tablespoon of it. I needed something that will tenderize the shrimp in this recipe, and I always have half-and-half on hand. The milk proteins tenderize the shrimp. So there. If you have coconut milk, use it. Otherwise: #RuthlessEfficiency, people! This recipe makes just enough sauce to serve the shrimp on top of sticky rice, but since they're not swimming in sauce, you might also want them over a salad, using the sauce as the salad dressing.   **SERVINGS: 4**

1. In a 6 × 3-inch round heatproof pan, combine the curry paste, coconut oil, half-and-half, fish sauce, soy sauce, ginger, and garlic. Whisk until well combined.

2. Add the shrimp and toss until well coated. Marinate at room temperature for 15 to 30 minutes.

3. Place the pan in the air fryer basket. Set the air fryer to 400°F for 5 minutes, stirring halfway through the cooking time.

4. Transfer the shrimp to a serving bowl or platter. Garnish with the basil and cilantro.

EGG-FREE, NUT-FREE, LOW-CARB

PREP TIME: 15 MINUTES
MARINATING TIME: 15 MINUTES
COOK TIME: 5 MINUTES
ACTIVE TIME: 15 MINUTES
TOTAL TIME: 35 MINUTES
COOK TEMPERATURE: 400°F

1 to 2 tablespoons Thai green curry paste

2 tablespoons coconut oil, melted

1 tablespoon half-and-half or coconut milk

1 teaspoon fish sauce

1 teaspoon soy sauce

1 teaspoon minced fresh ginger

1 clove garlic, minced

1 pound jumbo raw shrimp (21 to 25 count), peeled and deveined

¼ cup chopped fresh Thai basil or sweet basil

¼ cup chopped fresh cilantro

ONE-POT SHRIMP FRIED RICE

NUT-FREE, DAIRY-FREE

Okay people, you must try this recipe. It's weird-sounding but great-tasting and super-easy to make. And a great way to use up leftover rice as well. Add a little green vegetable or the shishito peppers on page 37 on the side, and you're all set for a colorful, tasty dinner. **SERVINGS: 4**

PREP TIME: 10 MINUTES

COOK TIME: 25 MINUTES

ACTIVE TIME: 20 MINUTES

TOTAL TIME: 35 MINUTES

COOK TEMPERATURE: 350°F

For the Shrimp

- 1 teaspoon cornstarch
- ½ teaspoon kosher salt
- ¼ teaspoon black pepper
- 1 pound jumbo raw shrimp (21 to 25 count), peeled and deveined

For the Rice

- 2 cups cold cooked rice
- 1 cup frozen peas and carrots, thawed
- ¼ cup chopped green onions (white and green parts)
- 3 tablespoons toasted sesame oil
- 1 tablespoon soy sauce
- ½ teaspoon kosher salt
- 1 teaspoon black pepper

For the Eggs

- 2 large eggs, beaten
- ¼ teaspoon kosher salt
- ¼ teaspoon black pepper

1. **For the shrimp:** In a small bowl, whisk together the cornstarch, salt, and pepper until well combined. Place the shrimp in a large bowl and sprinkle the seasoned cornstarch over. Toss until well coated; set aside.

2. **For the rice:** In a 6 × 3-inch round heatproof pan, combine the rice, peas and carrots, green onions, sesame oil, soy sauce, salt, and pepper. Toss and stir until well combined.

3. Place the pan in the air fryer basket. Set the air fryer to 350°F for 15 minutes, stirring and tossing the rice halfway through the cooking time.

4. Place the shrimp on top of the rice. Set the air fryer to 350°F for 5 minutes.

5. **Meanwhile, for the eggs:** In a medium bowl, beat the eggs with the salt and pepper.

6. Open the air fryer and pour the eggs over the shrimp and rice mixture. Set the air fryer to 350°F for 5 minutes.

7. Remove the pan from the air fryer. Stir to break up the rice and mix in the eggs and shrimp.

SALMON CROQUETTES

I like meals that can be put together with things from your pantry, mainly because I'm a terrible planner. If you keep a few pouches of salmon around, you should have almost everything else you need to make these croquettes. To make them keto/low carb or grain-free, substitute crushed pork rinds for the bread crumbs, and you should be good to go.   **SERVINGS: 2**

GRAIN-FREE, GLUTEN-FREE, NUT-FREE, DAIRY-FREE, PALEO, LOW-CARB

PREP TIME: 10 MINUTES

COOK TIME: 15 MINUTES

ACTIVE TIME: 10 MINUTES

TOTAL TIME: 25 MINUTES

COOK TEMPERATURE: 400°F

1. In a large bowl, combine the salmon, egg, bread crumbs, green onion, dillweed, salt, and pepper. Gently mix until well combined. Form into 4 patties. Lightly mist both sides of the patties with olive oil spray.

2. Spray the air fryer basket with olive oil spray. Arrange the patties in the air fryer basket. Set the air fryer to 400°F for 15 minutes, turning the patties and spraying both sides with more oil halfway through the cooking time. When done, the patties should be golden brown and crisp.

3. Serve the hot croquettes with lemon wedges.

- 2 (5-ounce) pouches wild-caught pink salmon
- 1 large egg, beaten
- ¼ cup panko bread crumbs or crushed pork rinds
- 1 green onion (white and light green parts), finely chopped
- 1 teaspoon dried dillweed
- ½ teaspoon kosher salt
- ½ teaspoon black pepper
- Olive oil spray
- Lemon wedges, for serving

PESTO FISH PIE

It may sound like an odd combination of ingredients, but this is a simple, yet colorful dish. The puff pastry makes it look quite elegant. Okay, I'll be honest. It looks elegant if my husband, Roger, does it. If I do it, it's like you let a small, clumsy child play with puff pastry—but hey, it's puff pastry, so it still doesn't look too bad! Most importantly, though, it tastes good.   **SERVINGS: 4**

EGG-FREE, SOY-FREE

PREP TIME: 15 MINUTES
COOK TIME: 15 MINUTES
ACTIVE TIME: 15 MINUTES
STANDING TIME: 5 MINUTES
TOTAL TIME: 35 MINUTES
COOK TEMPERATURE: 400°F

1. In a small bowl, combine the pesto, half-and-half, Parmesan, salt, and pepper. Stir until well combined; set aside.

2. Spray a 7 × 3-inch round heatproof pan with vegetable oil spray. Arrange the spinach evenly across the bottom of the pan. Top with the fish and tomatoes. Pour the pesto mixture evenly over everything.

3. On a lightly floured surface, roll the puff pastry sheet into a circle. Place the pastry on top of the pan and tuck it in around the edges of the pan. (Or, do what I do and stretch it with your hands and then pat it into place.)

4. Place the pan in the air fryer basket. Set the air fryer to 400°F for 15 minutes, or until the pastry is well browned. Let stand 5 minutes before serving.

- 2 tablespoons prepared pesto
- ¼ cup half-and-half
- ¼ cup grated Parmesan cheese
- 1 teaspoon kosher salt
- 1 teaspoon black pepper
- Vegetable oil spray
- 1 (10-ounce) package frozen chopped spinach, thawed and squeezed dry
- 1 pound firm white fish, cut into 2-inch chunks
- ½ cup cherry tomatoes, quartered
- All-purpose flour
- ½ sheet frozen puff pastry (from a 17.3-ounce package), thawed

SOUTH INDIAN FRIED FISH (MEEN VARUVAL)

GRAIN-FREE, GLUTEN-FREE,
EGG-FREE, NUT-FREE,
SOY-FREE, DAIRY-FREE,
PALEO, LOW-CARB

PREP TIME: 10 MINUTES
MARINATING TIME: 10 MINUTES
COOK TIME: 8 MINUTES
ACTIVE TIME: 10 MINUTES
TOTAL TIME: 30 MINUTES
COOK TEMPERATURE: 325°F/400°F

Recently we led a TwoSleevers culinary tour in South India. Yes, a tour whose sole purpose is to EAT—doesn't that just sound like heaven? One of the dishes I got to enjoy once again was *meen varuval*, or fried fish. Traditionally, this is shallow-fried and made with a spice paste that is quite thick. In an air fryer, that doesn't work so well as spices bloom and get even more intense under air fryer heat. So, I made a thinner paste and used it as a marinade. So this very simple recipe just shines, either by itself as a low-carb dish, or with a side of rice. You could also serve a side salad for an easy summertime supper.   **SERVINGS: 4**

1. In a large bowl, combine the oil, lime juice, ginger, garlic, turmeric, salt, and cayenne. Stir until well combined; set aside.

2. Cut each tilapia fillet into three or four equal-size pieces. Add the fish to the bowl and gently mix until all of the fish is coated in the marinade. Marinate for 10 to 15 minutes at room temperature. (Don't marinate any longer or the acid in the lime juice will "cook" the fish.)

3. Spray the air fryer basket with olive oil spray. Place the fish in the basket and spray the fish. Set the air fryer to 325°F for 3 minutes to partially cook the fish. Set the air fryer to 400°F for 5 minutes to finish cooking and crisp up the fish. (Thinner pieces of fish will cook faster so you may want to check at the 3-minute mark of the second cooking time and remove those that are cooked through, and then add them back toward the end of the second cooking time to crisp.)

4. Carefully remove the fish from the basket. Serve hot, with lemon wedges if desired.

2 tablespoons olive oil

2 tablespoons fresh lime or lemon juice

1 teaspoon minced fresh ginger

1 clove garlic, minced

1 teaspoon ground turmeric

½ teaspoon kosher salt

¼ to ½ teaspoon cayenne pepper

1 pound tilapia fillets (2 to 3 fillets)

Olive oil spray

Lime or lemon wedges (optional)

SEAFOOD

TANDOORI SHRIMP

You'll be surprised how easy it is to make an authentic-tasting tandoori shrimp with just a few ingredients. But your shrimp won't be that awful bright red color because—unlike as they do at restaurants—you aren't adding artificial food coloring. But yours will be at least as delicious, if not more so.   **SERVINGS: 4**

1. In a large bowl, combine the shrimp, ginger, garlic, cilantro, turmeric, garam masala, paprika, salt, and cayenne. Toss well to coat. Add the oil or ghee and toss again. Marinate at room temperature for 15 minutes, or cover and refrigerate for up to 8 hours.

2. Place the shrimp in a single layer in the air fryer basket. Set the air fryer to 325°F for 6 minutes. Transfer the shrimp to a serving platter. Cover and let the shrimp finish cooking in the residual heat, about 5 minutes.

3. Sprinkle the shrimp with the lemon juice and toss to coat. Garnish with additional cilantro and serve.

PREP TIME: 10 MINUTES
MARINATING TIME: 15 MINUTES
COOK TIME: 6 MINUTES
ACTIVE TIME: 10 MINUTES
STANDING TIME: 5 MINUTES
TOTAL TIME: 35 MINUTES
COOK TEMPERATURE: 325°F

- 1 pound jumbo raw shrimp (21 to 25 count), peeled and deveined
- 1 tablespoon minced fresh ginger
- 3 cloves garlic, minced
- ¼ cup chopped fresh cilantro or parsley, plus more for garnish
- 1 teaspoon ground turmeric
- 1 teaspoon Garam Masala (page 183)
- 1 teaspoon smoked paprika
- 1 teaspoon kosher salt
- ½ to 1 teaspoon cayenne pepper
- 2 tablespoons olive oil (for Paleo) or melted ghee
- 2 teaspoons fresh lemon juice

SCALLOPS GRATINÉ WITH PARMESAN

GRAIN-FREE, GLUTEN-FREE,
EGG-FREE, NUT-FREE,
SOY-FREE, LOW-CARB

This is an easy pour-and-cook recipe that you can make with bread crumbs or—for a gluten-free or keto option—pork rinds. You could also just double the Parmesan in the topping and skip the bread crumbs altogether. That last squirt of lemon juice from the wedges, however, is not to be skipped. The bit of tanginess is a wonderful complement to these easy, cheesy scallops.   **SERVINGS: 2**

PREP TIME: 10 MINUTES

COOK TIME: 9 MINUTES

ACTIVE TIME: 10 MINUTES

TOTAL TIME: 20 MINUTES

COOK TEMPERATURE: 325°F/400°F

1. **For the scallops:** In a 6 × 2-inch round heatproof pan, combine the half-and-half, cheese, green onions, parsley, garlic, salt, and pepper. Stir in the scallops.

2. **For the topping:** In a small bowl, combine the pork rinds or bread crumbs and cheese. Sprinkle evenly over the scallops. Spray the topping with vegetable oil spray.

3. Place the pan in the air fryer basket. Set the air fryer to 325°F for 6 minutes. Set the air fryer to 400°F for 3 minutes until the topping has browned.

4. **To serve:** Squeeze the lemon wedges over the gratin and serve with crusty French bread, if desired.

For the Scallops

- ½ cup half-and-half
- ½ cup grated Parmesan cheese
- ¼ cup thinly sliced green onions
- ¼ cup chopped fresh parsley
- 3 cloves garlic, minced
- ½ teaspoon kosher salt
- ½ teaspoon black pepper
- 1 pound sea scallops

For the Topping

- ¼ cup crushed pork rinds or panko bread crumbs
- ¼ cup grated Parmesan cheese
- Vegetable oil spray

For Serving

- Lemon wedges
- Crusty French bread (optional)

BEEF, &

PORK LAMB

BAKED KIBBEH

Traditional kibbeh, a Lebanese dish is made of bulgur, meat, and spices, is deep-fried. It is also terribly fiddly to make because you're essentially precooking two different types of ground lamb, and then you're making a shell with one, and then filling the shell with the other lamb, and while I am contemplating all these steps, I find myself thinking of something a lot simpler to make! So, I vastly simplified the traditional recipe to use only nuts and onions for the filling. All of the taste, but without the fiddly steps. **SERVINGS: 4**

EGG-FREE, SOY-FREE, DAIRY-FREE

PREP TIME: 15 MINUTES
COOK TIME: 28 MINUTES
ACTIVE TIME: 15 MINUTES
TOTAL TIME: 43 MINUTES
COOK TEMPERATURE: 400°F/350°F

1 cup bulgur

2 medium onions, thinly sliced

½ cup pine nuts

2 tablespoons vegetable oil

2 teaspoons kosher salt
Vegetable oil spray

1 pound ground lamb

4 teaspoons Lebanese Seven-Spice Mix (page 186)

1 teaspoon ground cumin
Tzatziki (page 95), for serving

1. Rinse the bulgur well. Cover with cold water and let stand while you get the rest of the ingredients together.

2. In a small bowl, combine the onions, pine nuts, oil, and 1 teaspoon of the salt. Spray a 7 × 3-inch round heatproof pan with vegetable oil spray. Place the onion mixture in the pan and place the pan in the air fryer basket. Set the air fryer to 400°F for 8 minutes, stirring halfway through the cooking time.

3. Meanwhile, in a stand mixer fitted with a paddle attachment, combine the drained bulgur, lamb, spice mix, cumin, and remaining 1 teaspoon salt. Beat until you have a smooth, sticky mixture.

4. Remove the pan with the onion mixture from the air fryer and transfer the mixture to a small bowl.

5. Spray the sides of the pan with oil spray. Spread half of the lamb mixture in the bottom of the pan. Top with all of the onion mixture. Top with the remaining lamb mixture, spreading to the sides of the pan.

6. Place the pan in the air fryer basket. Set the air fryer to 350°F for 20 minutes, or until lamb is browned and crisp. Serve with tzatziki.

CAJUN BACON PORK LOIN FILLET

GRAIN-FREE, GLUTEN-FREE, EGG-FREE, NUT-FREE, DAIRY-FREE, PALEO, LOW-CARB

Pork loin, pork tenderloin, pork loin fillet—what's the difference? I'm no butcher, but as a cook I will tell you a pork loin and a pork tenderloin do not cook at all alike, nor do they taste the same. This recipe calls for a pork loin fillet (aka pork tenderloin)—one of those pieces of pork that comes in a plastic tube-like package. It's a fairly dry piece of meat, so do not overcook. The bacon helps keep it a little moist as well, but you definitely want a meat thermometer for this recipe. It may look simple, but it is absolutely delicious. **SERVINGS: 6**

PREP TIME: 10 MINUTES
MARINATING TIME: 1 HOUR
COOK TIME: 20 MINUTES
ACTIVE TIME: 10 MINUTES
STANDING TIME: 10 MINUTES
TOTAL TIME: 1 HOUR 40 MINUTES
COOK TEMPERATURE: 350°F/400°F

1½ pounds pork loin fillet or pork tenderloin

3 tablespoons olive oil

2 tablespoons Cajun Spice Mix (page 182 or store-bought)

Salt (see Note)

6 slices bacon

Olive oil spray

1. Cut the pork in half so that it will fit in the air fryer basket.

2. Place both pieces of meat in a resealable plastic bag. Add the oil, Cajun seasoning, and salt to taste, if using. Seal the bag and massage to coat all of the meat with the oil and seasonings. Marinate in the refrigerator for at least 1 hour or up to 24 hours.

3. Remove the pork from the bag and wrap 3 bacon slices around each piece. Spray the air fryer basket with olive oil spray. Place the meat in the air fryer. Set the air fryer to 350°F for 15 minutes. Increase the temperature to 400°F for 5 minutes. Use a meat thermometer to ensure the meat has reached an internal temperature of 145°F.

4. Let the meat rest for 10 minutes. Slice into 6 medallions and serve.

NOTE

★ Use salt only if your Cajun seasoning does not contain any salt.

CHIPOTLE STEAK TACOS

Although I have written this recipe to use the beefy filling in tacos, there's nothing preventing you from serving the filling on a salad, over rice, with potatoes, or any other way you choose. The chipotles give it a lovely, smoky taste. Just note that we are asking for a few chipotles from the can, not one whole can! **SERVINGS: 4**

1. **For the filling:** Place the beef strips in a resealable plastic bag. In a blender or food processor, combine the water, olive oil, onion, garlic, chipotle chile and adobo sauce, chile powder, cumin, oregano, salt, and pepper. Blend until smooth. Pour the marinade over the meat. Seal the bag and massage to coat. Marinate at room temperature for 30 minutes or in the refrigerator for up to 24 hours.

2. Using tongs, remove the beef strips from the bag (discard the marinade) and lay them flat in the air fryer basket, minimizing overlap as much as possible. (You may have to cook the beef in two batches.) Set the air fryer to 400°F for 8 minutes, turning the beef strips halfway through the cooking time.

3. **To serve:** Divide the meat among the lettuce or tortillas and top with cheese and salsa.

GRAIN-FREE, GLUTEN-FREE, EGG-FREE, NUT-FREE, SOY-FREE, LOW-CARB

PREP TIME: 15 MINUTES
MARINATING TIME: 30 MINUTES
COOK TIME: 8 MINUTES
ACTIVE TIME: 15 MINUTES
TOTAL TIME: 53 MINUTES
COOK TEMPERATURE: 400°F

For the Beef Filling

- 1½ pounds flank steak, thinly sliced into long strips
- 2 tablespoons water
- 1 tablespoon olive oil
- 1 small red onion, diced
- 2 cloves garlic, crushed and peeled
- 1 canned chipotle chile in adobo sauce, plus 1 tablespoon adobo sauce from the can
- 1 tablespoon ancho chile powder
- 1 teaspoon ground cumin
- 1 teaspoon dried oregano
- 1½ teaspoons kosher salt
- ½ teaspoon black pepper

For Serving

- 8 lettuce leaves; or (6-inch) flour tortillas, warmed
- ½ cup crumbled cotija cheese
- 1 cup prepared salsa

GERMAN ROULADEN–STYLE STEAK

GRAIN-FREE, GLUTEN-FREE, EGG-FREE, NUT-FREE, SOY-FREE, LOW-CARB

I mean, meat and bacon, along with other yummies, rolled up into a cute little package—how can you resist? A typical roulade, steak rolled with a savory filling, involves a long, slow braise. This version gives you an entirely new dish, albeit with the same ingredients. I don't pound the steak at all; I cut it in half horizontally, and then use the other half for the Italian Steak Rolls on page 136. **SERVINGS: 4**

PREP TIME: 20 MINUTES
COOK TIME: 15 MINUTES
ACTIVE TIME: 20 MINUTES
STANDING TIME: 10 MINUTES
TOTAL TIME: 45 MINUTES
COOK TEMPERATURE: 400°F

1. **For the sauce:** In a small bowl, mix together the onions with salt and pepper to taste. Place the onions in the air fryer basket. Set the air fryer to 400°F for 6 minutes, or until the onions are softened and golden brown.

2. Set aside half of the onions to use in the rouladen. Place the rest in a small bowl and add the sour cream, tomato paste, parsley, ½ teaspoon salt, and ½ teaspoon pepper. Stir until well combined, adding 1 to 2 tablespoons of water, if necessary, to thin the sauce slightly. Set the sauce aside.

3. **For the rouladen:** Evenly spread the mustard over the meat. Sprinkle with the pepper. Top with the bacon slices, reserved onions, and parsley. Starting at the long end, roll up the steak as tightly as possible, ending seam side down. Use 2 or 3 wooden toothpicks to hold the roll together. Using a sharp knife, cut the roll in half so that it better fits in the air fryer basket.

4. Place the steak, seam side down, in the air fryer basket. Set the air fryer to 400°F for 9 minutes. Use a meat thermometer to ensure the steak has reached an internal temperature of 145°F. (It is critical to not overcook flank steak, so as to not toughen the meat.)

5. Let the steak rest for 10 minutes before cutting into slices. Serve with the sauce.

For the Onion Sauce

- 2 medium onions, cut into ½-inch-thick slices
- Kosher salt and black pepper
- ½ cup sour cream
- 1 tablespoon tomato paste
- 2 teaspoons chopped fresh parsley

For the Rouladen

- ¼ cup Dijon mustard
- 1 pound flank or skirt steak, ¼ to ½ inch thick
- 1 teaspoon black pepper
- 4 slices bacon
- ¼ cup chopped fresh parsley

HAM, CHICKEN & CHEESE CASSEROLE

GRAIN-FREE, GLUTEN-FREE, EGG-FREE, NUT-FREE, SOY-FREE, LOW-CARB

On the nights that you just can't even, but the people in your house still insist on being fed, here's an easy supper whose ingredients you can pick up at the deli on the way home. When you're done with the quick chop, spice, and cook, no one will know how easy it was to put this tasty delight together. Serve with a well-spiced vegetable side to offset the casserole's creamy, salty flavors.

SERVINGS: 4 TO 6

PREP TIME: 15 MINUTES
COOK TIME: 15 MINUTES
ACTIVE TIME: 15 MINUTES
TOTAL TIME: 30 MINUTES
COOK TEMPERATURE: 350°F

1. In a large bowl, combine the chicken, ham, pepper, nutmeg, and half-and-half. Stir to combine.

2. Spray a 6 × 3-inch round heatproof pan with vegetable oil spray. Place half of the chicken mixture in the pan. Layer with 3 slices of the cheese. Top with the remaining chicken mixture. Top with remaining cheese.

3. Place the pan in the air fryer basket. Set the air fryer to 350°F for 15 minutes, or until the casserole is bubbling.

- 2 cups diced cooked chicken
- 1 cup diced ham
- ½ teaspoon black pepper
- ¼ teaspoon ground nutmeg
- ½ cup half-and-half
  Vegetable oil spray
- 6 slices Swiss cheese

135

BEEF, PORK & LAMB

ITALIAN STEAK ROLLS

This roll is so colorful with its green spinach, red peppers, and gooey white mozzarella—the same colors as the Italian flag. A coincidence? I think not! (Here are the benefits of having a kid who was obsessed with national flags—I actually remember some of them.) More importantly though, this is a great way to get meat, cheese, and veggies all in one swoop. I suggest you buy a flank steak and slice it in half horizontally (so you don't have to pound it), and use the other half for the German Rouladen–Style Steak on page 134. **SERVINGS: 4**

GRAIN-FREE, GLUTEN-FREE, EGG-FREE, NUT-FREE, SOY-FREE, LOW-CARB

PREP TIME: 20 MINUTES
MARINATING TIME: 30 MINUTES
COOK TIME: 9 MINUTES
ACTIVE TIME: 20 MINUTES
STANDING TIME: 10 MINUTES
TOTAL TIME: 1 HOUR 10 MINUTES
COOK TEMPERATURE: 400°F

1. In a large bowl, combine the oil, garlic, Italian seasoning, salt, and pepper. Whisk to combine. Add the steak to the bowl, turning to ensure the entire steak is covered with the seasonings. Cover and marinate at room temperature for 30 minutes or in the refrigerator for up to 24 hours.

2. Lay the steak on a flat surface. Spread the spinach evenly over the steak, leaving a ¼-inch border at the edge. Evenly top each steak with the red pepper and cheese.

3. Starting at a long end, roll up the steak as tightly as possible, ending seam side down. Use 2 or 3 wooden toothpicks to hold the roll together. Using a sharp knife, cut the roll in half so that it better fits in the air fryer basket.

4. Place the steak roll, seam side down, in the air fryer basket. Set the air fryer to 400°F for 9 minutes. Use a meat thermometer to ensure the steak has reached an internal temperature of 145°F. (It is critical to not overcook flank steak, so as to not toughen the meat.)

5. Let the steak rest for 10 minutes before cutting into slices to serve.

- 1 tablespoon vegetable oil
- 2 cloves garlic, minced
- 2 teaspoons dried Italian seasoning
- 1 teaspoon kosher salt
- 1 teaspoon black pepper
- 1 pound flank or skirt steak, ¼ to ½ inch thick
- 1 (10-ounce) package frozen spinach, thawed and squeezed dry
- ½ cup diced jarred roasted red pepper
- 1 cup shredded mozzarella cheese

KHEEMA BURGERS

Kheema is a very popular Indian and Pakistani dish, and with good reason. The authentic Indian dish comes together quickly, tastes complex, and can be made at home very quickly. Of course, making a burger out of it is not that authentic. But why not, I ask you? I serve the burgers with a sour cream–based raita to add a little tang. Keep in mind that not all burgers come in buns, so be creative. **SERVINGS: 4**

GRAIN-FREE, GLUTEN-FREE, NUT-FREE, SOY-FREE, LOW-CARB

PREP TIME: 15 MINUTES
COOK TIME: 12 MINUTES
ACTIVE TIME: 15 MINUTES
TOTAL TIME: 27 MINUTES
COOK TEMPERATURE: 350°F

1. **For the burgers:** In a large bowl, combine the ground beef, eggs, onion, cilantro, ginger, garlic, garam masala, turmeric, cinnamon, cardamom, salt, and cayenne. Gently mix until ingredients are thoroughly combined.

2. Divide the meat into four portions and form into round patties. Make a slight depression in the middle of each patty with your thumb to prevent them from puffing up into a dome shape while cooking.

3. Place the patties in the air fryer basket. Set the air fryer to 350°F for 12 minutes. Use a meat thermometer to ensure the burgers have reached an internal temperature of 160°F (for medium).

4. **Meanwhile, for the sauce:** In a small bowl, combine the cucumber, sour cream, salt, and pepper.

5. **To serve:** Place the burgers on the lettuce, buns, or naan and top with the sauce.

NOTE

★ If you have a small air fryer, you may need to cook the burgers in two batches, or you could use a rack to elevate two burgers over the other two, and switch places halfway through cooking.

For the Burgers

- 1 pound 85% lean ground beef or ground lamb
- 2 large eggs, lightly beaten
- 1 medium yellow onion, diced
- ¼ cup chopped fresh cilantro
- 1 tablespoon minced fresh ginger
- 3 cloves garlic, minced
- 2 teaspoons Garam Masala (page 183)
- 1 teaspoon ground turmeric
- ½ teaspoon ground cinnamon
- ⅛ teaspoon ground cardamom
- 1 teaspoon kosher salt
- 1 teaspoon cayenne pepper

For the Raita Sauce

- 1 cup grated cucumber
- ½ cup sour cream
- ¼ teaspoon kosher salt
- ¼ teaspoon black pepper

For Serving

- 4 lettuce leaves, hamburger buns, or naan breads

KOREAN BEEF
TACOS

LAMB CHOPS WITH HORSERADISH SAUCE

If you marinate the chops ahead of time, this elegant little dish comes together very quickly. Use loin lamb chops for this recipe. You can either buy a prepared horseradish cream sauce or whip one up with the simple recipe below. For these chops, you use the sauce as a glaze as well as a serving sauce.   **SERVINGS: 4**

PREP TIME: 10 MINUTES
MARINATING TIME: 30 MINUTES
COOK TIME: 13 MINUTES
ACTIVE TIME: 10 MINUTES
TOTAL TIME: 53 MINUTES
COOK TEMPERATURE: 325°F/400°F

1. **For the lamb:** Brush the lamb chops with the oil, rub with the garlic, and sprinkle with the salt and pepper. Marinate at room temperature for 30 minutes.

2. **Meanwhile, for the sauce:** In a medium bowl, combine the mayonnaise, mustard, horseradish, and sugar. Stir until well combined. Set aside half of the sauce for serving.

3. Spray the air fryer basket with vegetable oil spray and place the chops in the basket. Set the air fryer to 325°F for 10 minutes, turning the chops halfway through the cooking time.

4. Remove the chops from the air fryer and add to the bowl with the horseradish sauce, turning to coat with the sauce. Place the chops back in the air fryer basket. Set the air fryer to 400°F for 3 minutes. Use a meat thermometer to ensure the meat has reached an internal temperature of 145°F (for medium-rare).

5. Serve the chops with the reserved horseradish sauce.

For the Lamb

- 4 lamb loin chops
- 2 tablespoons vegetable oil
- 1 clove garlic, minced
- ½ teaspoon kosher salt
- ½ teaspoon black pepper

For the Horseradish Cream Sauce

- ½ cup mayonnaise
- 1 tablespoon Dijon mustard
- 1 to 1½ tablespoons prepared horseradish
- 2 teaspoons sugar
- Vegetable oil spray

NIGERIAN PEANUT-CRUSTED FLANK STEAK (SUYA)

PREP TIME: 15 MINUTES
MARINATING TIME: 30 MINUTES
COOK TIME: 8 MINUTES
ACTIVE TIME: 15 MINUTES
TOTAL TIME: 53 MINUTES
COOK TEMPERATURE: 400°F

If you're anything like me, you *will* eat the suya spice-peanut mixture with a spoon when no one is looking. There's just something about it that is very addictive. When I first made this *suya*, or Nigerian peanut beef, I found myself sprinkling more and more of the seasoning on the beef. It is traditionally served with onions, as a snack. I make a salad or a whole low-carb meal out of the steak. It would also be great wrapped in lettuce, or just cut into smaller pieces and eaten with toothpicks alongside a nice cold drink.　**SERVINGS: 4**

For the Suya Spice Mix

- ¼ cup dry-roasted peanuts
- 1 teaspoon cumin seeds
- 1 teaspoon garlic powder
- 1 teaspoon smoked paprika
- ½ teaspoon ground ginger
- 1 teaspoon kosher salt
- ½ teaspoon cayenne pepper

For the Steak

- 1 pound flank steak
- 2 tablespoons vegetable oil

1. **For the spice mix:** In a clean coffee grinder or spice mill, combine the peanuts and cumin seeds. Process until you get a coarse powder. (Do not overprocess or you will wind up with peanut butter! Alternatively, you can grind the cumin with ⅓ cup ready-made peanut powder, such as PB2, instead of the peanuts.)

2. Pour the peanut mixture into a small bowl, add the garlic powder, paprika, ginger, salt, and cayenne, and stir to combine. This recipe makes about ½ cup suya spice mix. Store leftovers in an airtight container in a cool, dry place for up to 1 month.

3. **For the steak:** Cut the flank steak into ½-inch-thick slices, cutting against the grain and at a slight angle. Place the beef strips in a resealable plastic bag and add the oil and 2½ to 3 tablespoons of the spice mixture. Seal the bag and massage to coat all of the meat with the oil and spice mixture. Marinate at room temperature for 30 minutes or in the refrigerator for up to 24 hours.

4. Place the beef strips in the air fryer basket. Set the air fryer to 400°F for 8 minutes, turning the strips halfway through the cooking time.

5. Transfer the meat to a serving platter. Sprinkle with additional spice mix, if desired.

PHILLY CHEESESTEAKS

Meat, veggies, bread, and cheese all cooked in the air fryer? Yes, please. These sandwiches are simple but very filling. Besides, anything that has bread and cheese in it is a win as far as I'm concerned. If you have trouble slicing the meat thinly, try freezing the beef for 30 minutes. Me, I'm usually in too much of a hurry to do that. Serve with grilled vegetables instead of the rolls to make this low-carb. **SERVINGS: 2**

EGG-FREE, NUT-FREE

PREP TIME: 20 MINUTES
COOK TIME: 20 MINUTES
ACTIVE TIME: 20 MINUTES
TOTAL TIME: 40 MINUTES
COOK TEMPERATURE: 400°F

1. In a medium bowl, combine the meat, Worcestershire sauce, soy sauce, and salt and pepper to taste. Toss until the meat is evenly coated; set aside.

2. In another medium bowl, combine the onion, bell pepper, and oil. Season to taste with salt and pepper. Toss until the vegetables are evenly coated.

3. Place the meat and vegetables in the air fryer basket. Set the air fryer to 400°F for 15 minutes, or until the meat and vegetables are cooked through, tossing once or twice. Transfer the meat and vegetables to a plate and cover lightly with foil; set aside.

4. If using butter: Spread the insides of the rolls with the butter. Place the rolls in the air fryer basket, top sides down. Set the air fryer to 400°F for 3 minutes, or until the rolls are lightly toasted. Remove the rolls from the basket.

5. Divide the meat and vegetables between the two rolls. Top each with cheese. Place in the air fryer basket. Set the air fryer to 400°F for 2 minutes, or until the cheese melts.

- 12 ounces boneless rib-eye steak, sliced as thinly as possible
- ½ teaspoon Worcestershire sauce
- ½ teaspoon soy sauce

  Kosher salt and black pepper
- ½ small onion, halved and thinly sliced
- ½ green bell pepper, stemmed, seeded, and thinly sliced
- 1 tablespoon vegetable oil
- 1 tablespoon butter, softened (optional)
- 2 soft hoagie rolls, split three-fourths of the way through
- 2 slices provolone cheese, halved

PORCHETTA-STYLE PORK CHOPS

GRAIN-FREE, GLUTEN-FREE,
EGG-FREE, DAIRY-FREE,
PALEO, LOW-CARB

Pork chops cook up crispy on the outside and juicy on the inside in the air fryer. The spice rub, with its mix of fennel seeds and herbs, is easy and tasty. The fresh herbs crushed into the olive oil release a fresh, herby aroma as the chops cook, making this dish very satisfying on all counts. **SERVINGS: 2**

PREP TIME: 10 MINUTES
COOK TIME: 15 MINUTES
ACTIVE TIME: 10 MINUTES
TOTAL TIME: 25 MINUTES
COOK TEMPERATURE: 375°F

1. In a small bowl, combine the olive oil, zest, garlic, rosemary, sage, fennel seeds, red pepper, salt, and black pepper. Stir, crushing the herbs with the back of a spoon, until a paste forms (adding a little more olive oil if necessary). Spread the seasoning mix on both sides of the pork chops.

2. Place the chops in the air fryer basket. Set the air fryer to 375°F for 15 minutes. Use a meat thermometer to ensure the chops have reached an internal temperature of 145°F.

1 tablespoon extra-virgin olive oil

Grated zest of 1 lemon

2 cloves garlic, minced

2 teaspoons chopped fresh rosemary

1 teaspoon finely chopped fresh sage

1 teaspoon fennel seeds, lightly crushed

¼ to ½ teaspoon red pepper flakes

1 teaspoon kosher salt

1 teaspoon black pepper

2 (8-ounce) center-cut bone-in pork chops, about 1 inch thick

SPICY CHICKEN-FRIED STEAK WITH PEPPERCORN GRAVY

You can't live in Texas without running into chicken-fried steak at every corner. I wasn't sure these would work in the air fryer, since breaded things can be a little hit and miss. But this one is in the hit column. **SERVINGS: 2**

NUT-FREE, SOY-FREE

PREP TIME: 20 MINUTES
COOK TIME: 8 MINUTES
ACTIVE TIME: 20 MINUTES
TOTAL TIME: 45 MINUTES
COOK TEMPERATURE: 400°F

1. **For the steaks:** Cut the steaks in half if needed to fit in the air fryer basket; set aside. In a shallow bowl, whisk the flour, sage, paprika, onion powder, garlic powder, cayenne, 1 teaspoon salt, and 1 teaspoon pepper.

2. In a separate shallow bowl, whisk together the buttermilk, egg, and hot pepper sauce until combined.

3. Using a paper towel, pat the steaks dry. Season to taste with salt and pepper. Allow to stand for 5 minutes, then pat dry again.

4. Dredge the steaks in the flour mixture, shaking off any excess; then dip in the buttermilk mixture, allowing excess to drip off. Dredge once more in the flour mixture, shaking off excess. Place the breaded steaks on a baking sheet and press any of the remaining flour mixture onto the steaks, making sure that each steak is completely coated. Let stand for 10 minutes.

5. Place the steaks in the air fryer basket. Lightly coat with vegetable oil spray. Set the air fryer to 400°F for 8 minutes, carefully turning the steaks halfway through the cooking time and coating the other side with the oil spray. Use a meat thermometer to ensure the steaks have reached an internal temperature of 145°F.

6. **Meanwhile, for the gravy:** In a small saucepan, melt the butter over low heat. Add the flour, garlic salt, kosher salt, and cracked pepper and whisk until smooth. Slowly add the milk and cream while continuing to whisk. Turn the heat to medium and cook, whisking occasionally, until the gravy thickens. Serve the steaks topped with the gravy.

For the Steaks

- 2 beef cube steaks (5 to 6 ounces each)
- ¾ cup all-purpose flour
- 2 teaspoons crumbled dried sage
- ½ teaspoon smoked paprika
- ½ teaspoon onion powder
- ½ teaspoon garlic powder
- ¼ teaspoon cayenne pepper
- Kosher salt and black pepper
- ¾ cup buttermilk
- 1 large egg
- 1 teaspoon hot pepper sauce
- Vegetable oil spray

For the Gravy

- 2 tablespoons butter
- 2 tablespoons all-purpose flour
- ¼ teaspoon garlic salt
- ½ teaspoon kosher salt
- ½ teaspoon cracked black pepper
- 1 cup whole milk
- ½ cup heavy whipping cream

SPICY FLANK STEAK WITH ZHOUG

Zh—what? It's *zhoug,* pronounced "zoog." Or, as I call it: spicy deliciousness to the max. Calling the Middle Eastern hot sauce a cilantro pesto is a close approximation, but I will be the first to admit that that name does this herby, spicy mix a great disservice. Make lots of the sauce and use it with everything. I have often used it to make butter and zhoug sandwiches. Flank steak, if overcooked, can get really dry, so err on the side of undercooking the steak a little. **SERVINGS: 4**

1. **For the marinade and steak:** In a small bowl, whisk together the beer, lemon juice, garlic, olive oil, sriracha, brown sugar, cumin, paprika, salt, and pepper. Place the steak in a large resealable plastic bag. Pour the marinade over the steak, seal the bag, and massage the steak to coat. Marinate in the refrigerator for 1 hour or up to 24 hours, turning the bag occasionally.

2. **Meanwhile, for the zhoug:** In a food processor, combine the cilantro, garlic, jalapeños, cumin, coriander, and salt. Process until finely chopped. Add 2 tablespoons olive oil and pulse to form a loose paste, adding up to 2 tablespoons more olive oil if needed. Transfer the zhoug to a glass container. Cover and store in the refrigerator until 30 minutes before serving if marinating more than 1 hour.

3. Remove the steak from the marinade and discard the marinade. Place the steak in the air fryer basket and set the air fryer to 400°F for 8 minutes. Use a meat thermometer to ensure the steak has reached an internal temperature of 150°F (for medium).

4. Transfer the steak to a cutting board and let rest for 5 minutes. Slice the steak across the grain and serve with the zhoug.

GRAIN-FREE, EGG-FREE, NUT-FREE, SOY-FREE, DAIRY-FREE, LOW-CARB

PREP TIME: 20 MINUTES
MARINATING TIME: 1 HOUR
COOK TIME: 8 MINUTES
ACTIVE TIME: 20 MINUTES
TOTAL TIME: 1 HOUR 30 MINUTES
COOK TEMPERATURE: 400°F

For the Marinade and Steak

- ½ cup dark beer or orange juice
- ¼ cup fresh lemon juice
- 3 cloves garlic, minced
- 2 tablespoons extra-virgin olive oil
- 2 tablespoons sriracha
- 2 tablespoons brown sugar
- 2 teaspoons ground cumin
- 2 teaspoons smoked paprika
- 1 tablespoon kosher salt
- 1 teaspoon black pepper
- 1½ pounds flank steak, trimmed and cut into 3 pieces

For the Zhoug

- 1 cup packed fresh cilantro leaves
- 2 cloves garlic, peeled
- 2 jalapeño or serrano chiles, stemmed and coarsely chopped
- ½ teaspoon ground cumin
- ¼ teaspoon ground coriander
- ¼ teaspoon kosher salt
- 2 to 4 tablespoons extra-virgin olive oil

SWEET & SPICY COUNTRY-STYLE RIBS

GRAIN-FREE, GLUTEN-FREE,
EGG-FREE, NUT-FREE,
SOY-FREE, DAIRY-FREE

Sweet, spicy, porky, slurpy, messy ribs that taste good and cook fast—how does it get better than that? It doesn't. Serve with a vinegar-based coleslaw for a perfect Southern meal. **SERVINGS: 4**

PREP TIME: 10 MINUTES
COOK TIME: 25 MINUTES
ACTIVE TIME: 10 MINUTES
TOTAL TIME: 35 MINUTES
COOK TEMPERATURE: 350°F

1. In a small bowl, stir together the brown sugar, paprika, garlic powder, onion powder, dry mustard, cumin, salt, black pepper, and cayenne. Mix until well combined.

2. Pat the ribs dry with a paper towel. Generously sprinkle the rub evenly over both sides of the ribs and rub in with your fingers.

3. Place the ribs in the air fryer basket. Set the air fryer to 350°F for 15 minutes. Turn the ribs and brush with ½ cup of the barbecue sauce. Cook for an additional 10 minutes. Use a meat thermometer to ensure the pork has reached an internal temperature of 145°F.

4. Serve with remaining barbecue sauce.

2	tablespoons brown sugar
2	tablespoons smoked paprika
1	teaspoon garlic powder
1	teaspoon onion powder
1	teaspoon dry mustard
1	teaspoon ground cumin
1	teaspoon kosher salt
1	teaspoon black pepper
¼ to ½	teaspoon cayenne pepper
1½	pounds boneless country-style pork ribs
1	cup barbecue sauce

POBLANO CHEESEBURGERS WITH AVOCADO-CHIPOTLE MAYO

GRAIN-FREE, GLUTEN-FREE, NUT-FREE, SOY-FREE, LOW-CARB

PREP TIME: 30 MINUTES
COOK TIME: 27 MINUTES
ACTIVE TIME: 30 MINUTES
STANDING TIME: 5 MINUTES
TOTAL TIME: 1 HOUR
COOK TEMPERATURE: 375°F/350°F

Is there no end to the ways in which I will flavor and hack burgers? Probably not. Ground beef can be used in so much more than just tacos, chili, and plain burgers. This recipe is a great example of how just the right seasoning and spices can dress up a weeknight dinner. If you have a small air fryer, you may need to cook the burgers in two batches, or you could use a rack to elevate two burgers over the other two, and switch places halfway through cooking. The avocado-chipotle mayo is so yummy that you might want to make a double batch and use it with just about anything you can think of during the rest of the week. **SERVINGS: 4**

1. **For the burgers:** Brush the poblano pepper with a little bit of oil and place in the air fryer basket. Set the air fryer to 375°F for 15 minutes, turning the pepper halfway through the cooking time. When the pepper is soft, wrinkled, and charred, remove it from the air fryer and cover with a clean dish towel. Let stand for 5 minutes to steam. When the pepper is cool enough to handle, remove the skin, stem, and seeds and then dice the pepper.

2. In a large bowl, gently mix the diced poblano, ground beef, and garlic until well combined. Shape into four patties and season both sides with salt and pepper to taste. Make a slight depression in the middle of each patty with your thumb to prevent them from puffing up into a dome shape while cooking.

3. Arrange the patties in the air fryer basket. Set the air fryer to 350°F for 12 minutes. Place a slice of cheese on each burger during the last minute or two of the cooking time. Use a meat thermometer to ensure the burgers have reached an internal temperature of 160°F (for medium).

For the Burgers

- 1 poblano pepper

  Extra-virgin olive oil

- 1 pound 85% lean ground beef

- 2 cloves garlic, minced

  Kosher salt and black pepper

- 4 slices Monterey Jack cheese

For the Avocado-Chipotle Mayonnaise

- 1 small ripe avocado, pitted, peeled, and cut into chunks

- ½ cup mayonnaise

  Juice from ½ lime

- 2 canned chipotle peppers in adobo sauce, sliced in half lengthwise, seeded, and finely chopped

- 2 teaspoons chopped fresh cilantro

4. **Meanwhile, for the mayonnaise:** In a blender combine the avocado, mayonnaise, lime juice, chipotle peppers, and cilantro. Blend until smooth.

5. **To serve:** Slather some mayo on a lettuce leaf or a bottom bun. Top with a patty, then add the onion, tomato, and lettuce (and finish with the top bun if using).

NOTES

★ This recipe makes about 1 cup Avocado-Chipotle Mayonnaise. Store any remaining mayonnaise in the refrigerator for up to 1 week.

For Serving

4 lettuce leaves; or 4 hamburger buns, lightly toasted

1 red onion, sliced

Ripe tomatoes, sliced

Bibb lettuce

TACO MEATBALLS

Who doesn't like tacos? Who doesn't like meatballs? So, then, who doesn't like taco-seasoned meatballs? Probably everyone will love these, including those picky little family members.   **SERVINGS: 4**

1. **For the meatballs:** In the bowl of a stand mixer fitted with the paddle attachment, combine the ground beef, cheese, egg, onion, cilantro, garlic, taco seasoning, salt, and pepper. Mix on low speed until all of the ingredients are incorporated, 2 to 3 minutes.

2. Form the mixture into 12 meatballs and arrange in a single layer in the air fryer basket. Set the air fryer to 400°F for 10 minutes. Use a meat thermometer to ensure the meatballs have reached an internal temperature of 160°F (for medium).

3. **Meanwhile, for the sauce:** In a small bowl, combine the sour cream, salsa, and hot sauce. Stir until well combined.

4. Transfer the meatballs to a serving bowl. Ladle the sauce over the meatballs and serve.

GRAIN-FREE, GLUTEN-FREE, NUT-FREE, SOY-FREE, LOW-CARB

PREP TIME: 15 MINUTES
COOK TIME: 10 MINUTES
ACTIVE TIME: 15 MINUTES
TOTAL TIME: 25 MINUTES
COOK TEMPERATURE: 400°F

For the Meatballs

- 1 pound 85% lean ground beef
- ½ cup shredded Mexican cheese blend
- 1 large egg
- ¼ cup finely minced onion
- ¼ cup chopped fresh cilantro
- 3 cloves garlic, minced
- 2½ tablespoons taco seasoning
- 1 teaspoon kosher salt
- 1 teaspoon black pepper

For the Sauce

- ¼ cup sour cream
- ½ cup salsa
- 1 to 2 teaspoons Cholula hot sauce or Sriracha

WONTON MEATBALLS

I love, love, love wontons. But I don't always love the wrapping and rolling, especially now that my son Alex isn't at home anymore, as it was his job to wrap the wontons. So making wonton-inspired meatballs instead gets me all of the flavor with hardly any of the effort! **SERVINGS: 4**

NUT-FREE, DAIRY-FREE, LOW-CARB

PREP TIME: 15 MINUTES
COOK TIME: 10 MINUTES
ACTIVE TIME: 15 MINUTES
TOTAL TIME: 25 MINUTES
COOK TEMPERATURE: 350°F

1. In the bowl of a stand mixer fitted with the paddle attachment, combine the pork, eggs, green onions, cilantro, ginger, garlic, soy sauce, oyster sauce, salt, and pepper. Mix on low speed until all of the ingredients are incorporated, 2 to 3 minutes.

2. Form the mixture into 12 meatballs and arrange in a single layer in the air fryer basket. Set the air fryer to **350°F** for 10 minutes. Use a meat thermometer to ensure the meatballs have reached an internal temperature of 145°F.

3. Transfer the meatballs to a bowl and serve.

1	pound ground pork
2	large eggs
¼	cup chopped green onions (white and green parts)
¼	cup chopped fresh cilantro or parsley
1	tablespoon minced fresh ginger
3	cloves garlic, minced
2	teaspoons soy sauce
1	teaspoon oyster sauce
½	teaspoon kosher salt
1	teaspoon black pepper

DESS

ERTS

APPLE DUTCH BABY

Apples, batter, and warm spices like nutmeg and cinnamon—how could anyone not love this combination? The batter is light and fluffy and it all comes together with ease while still looking and tasting quite complex. Enjoy this puffy oven pancake as a dessert, a decadent breakfast, a light lunch, or just because.

SERVINGS: 2 TO 3

NUT-FREE, SOY-FREE, VEGETARIAN

PREP TIME: 20 MINUTES
STANDING TIME: 30 MINUTES
COOK TIME: 16 MINUTES
ACTIVE TIME: 20 MINUTES
TOTAL TIME: 1 HOUR 6 MINUTES
COOK TEMPERATURE: 400°F/350°F

1. **For the batter:** In a medium bowl, combine the eggs, flour, baking powder, sugar, and salt. Whisk lightly. While whisking continuously, slowly pour in the milk. Whisk in the melted butter, vanilla, and nutmeg. Let the batter stand for 30 minutes. (You can also cover and refrigerate overnight.)

2. **For the apples:** Place the butter in a 6 × 3-inch round heatproof pan. Place the pan in the air fryer basket. Set the air fryer to 400°F for 2 minutes. In a small bowl, combine 2 tablespoons of the sugar with the cinnamon and nutmeg and stir until well combined.

3. When the pan is hot and the butter is melted, brush some butter up the sides of the pan. Sprinkle the spiced sugar mixture over the butter. Arrange the apple slices in the pan in a single layer and sprinkle the remaining 2 tablespoons sugar over the apples. Set the air fryer to 400°F to 2 minutes, or until the mixture bubbles.

4. Gently pour the batter over the apples. Set the air fryer to 350°F for 12 minutes, or until the pancake is golden brown around the edges, the center is cooked through, and a toothpick emerges clean.

5. Serve immediately with ice cream, if desired.

For the Batter

- 2 large eggs
- ¼ cup all-purpose flour
- ¼ teaspoon baking powder
- 1½ teaspoons granulated sugar
- Pinch kosher salt
- ½ cup whole milk
- 1 tablespoon butter, melted
- ½ teaspoon pure vanilla extract
- ¼ teaspoon ground nutmeg

For the Apples

- 2 tablespoon butter
- 4 tablespoons granulated sugar
- ¼ teaspoon ground cinnamon
- ¼ teaspoon ground nutmeg
- 1 small tart apple (such as Granny Smith), peeled, cored, and sliced
- Vanilla ice cream (optional), for serving

BLUEBERRY–CREAM CHEESE BREAD PUDDING

NUT-FREE, SOY-FREE, VEGETARIAN

I know it may sound a little odd that I'm basically asking you to throw chunks of cream cheese willy-nilly into this dessert. Here's the thing: The cream cheese is going to melt and soften and just smoosh in here and there, and you'll taste its wonderful creaminess throughout the pudding. It contrasts well with the blueberry and lemon flavors and makes this a rich and decadent-but-easy dessert you can enjoy. **SERVINGS: 6**

PREP TIME: 15 MINUTES
COOK TIME: 70 MINUTES
ACTIVE TIME: 15 MINUTES
STANDING TIME: 10 MINUTES
TOTAL TIME: 1 HOUR 35 MINUTES
COOK TEMPERATURE: 400°F/350°F

1 cup light cream or half-and-half

4 large eggs

1/3 cup plus 3 tablespoons granulated sugar

1 teaspoon pure lemon extract

4 cups cubed croissants (4 to 5 croissants)

1 cup blueberries

4 ounces cream cheese, cut into small cubes

1. In a large bowl, combine the cream, eggs, the 1/3 cup sugar, and the extract. Whisk until well combined. Add the cubed croissants, blueberries, and cream cheese. Toss gently until everything is thoroughly combined; set aside.

2. Place a 3-cup Bundt pan in the air fryer basket. Preheat the air fryer to 400°F.

3. Sprinkle the remaining 3 tablespoons sugar in the bottom of the hot pan. Set the air fryer to 400°F for 10 minutes, or until the sugar caramelizes. Tip the pan to spread the caramel evenly across the bottom of the pan.

4. Remove the pan from the air fryer and pour in the bread mixture, distributing it evenly across the pan. Place the pan in the air fryer basket. Set the air fryer to 350°F for 60 minutes, or until the custard is set in the middle. Let stand for 10 minutes before unmolding onto a serving plate.

SPICED PEARS WITH HONEY-LEMON RICOTTA

GRAIN-FREE, GLUTEN-FREE, EGG-FREE, SOY-FREE, VEGETARIAN

This is a super-simple recipe that tastes very sophisticated. I love that you can make the honey-lemon ricotta ahead of time. That way, you can put in the pears to cook just as you sit down to dinner, and when you're done, you'll only need to top the sweetened ricotta with the warm pears. **SERVINGS: 4**

PREP TIME: 10 MINUTES
COOK TIME: 8 MINUTES
ACTIVE TIME: 10 MINUTES
TOTAL TIME: 20 MINUTES
COOK TEMPERATURE: 375°F

1. Peel each pear and cut in half lengthwise. Use a melon baller to scoop out the core. Place the pear halves in a medium bowl, add the melted butter, and toss. Add the brown sugar, ginger, and cardamom; toss to coat.

2. Place the pear halves, cut side down, in the air fryer basket. Set the air fryer to 375°F for 8 to 10 minutes, or until the pears are lightly browned and tender, but not mushy.

3. Meanwhile, in a medium bowl, combine the ricotta, honey, and almond and lemon extracts. Beat with an electric mixer on medium speed until the mixture is light and fluffy, about 1 minute.

4. To serve, divide the ricotta mixture among four small shallow bowls. Place a pear half, cut side up, on top of the cheese. Drizzle with additional honey and serve.

- 2 large Bartlett pears
- 3 tablespoons butter, melted
- 3 tablespoons brown sugar
- ½ teaspoon ground ginger
- ¼ teaspoon ground cardamom
- ½ cup whole-milk ricotta cheese
- 1 tablespoon honey, plus additional for drizzling
- 1 teaspoon pure almond extract
- 1 teaspoon pure lemon extract

INDIAN TOAST & MILK (SHAHI TUKDA)

Shahi tukda ("Shahi toast") is a traditional Indian dessert of deep-fried bread slices that are soaked in milk. So of course, I had to try to air fry the bread. But I didn't want you to have to use two different appliances, so I made the milk part in the air fryer too. You can of course thicken the milk on the stovetop instead. You want to give the toast enough time to soak up the sweet milk, but not so long that it turns to mush. (Although the mush tastes just as good!) **SERVINGS: 4**

1. In a 6×4-inch round heatproof pan, combine the condensed milk, evaporated milk, half-and-half, cardamom, and saffron. Stir until well combined.

2. Place the pan in the air fryer basket. Set the air fryer to 350°F for 15 minutes, stirring halfway through the cooking time. Remove the sweetened milk from the air fryer and set aside.

3. Cut each slice of bread into two triangles. Brush each side with ghee. Place the bread in the air fryer basket. Set the air fryer to 350°F for 5 minutes or until golden brown and toasty.

4. Remove the bread from the air fryer. Arrange two triangles in each of four wide, shallow bowls. Pour the hot milk mixture on top of the bread and let soak for 30 minutes.

5. Garnish with pistachios if using, and sprinkle with additional cardamom.

NUT-FREE, SOY-FREE, VEGETARIAN

PREP TIME: 10 MINUTES
COOK TIME: 20 MINUTES
ACTIVE TIME: 10 MINUTES
STANDING TIME: 30 MINUTES
TOTAL TIME: 1 HOUR
COOK TEMPERATURE: 350°F

1 cup sweetened condensed milk

1 cup evaporated milk

1 cup half-and-half

1 teaspoon ground cardamom, plus additional for garnish

1 pinch saffron threads

4 slices white bread

2 to 3 tablespoons ghee or butter, softened

2 tablespoons crushed pistachios, for garnish (optional)

MAPLE-PECAN TART WITH SEA SALT

EGG-FREE, SOY-FREE, VEGETARIAN

This was so so so very good that when I first made it I immediately invited friends over to eat it—not only because I wanted them to experience it, but also because I was afraid Roger and I would have eaten the whole tart by ourselves! It's very rich, so small pieces will likely suffice for everyone.   **SERVINGS: 8**

PREP TIME: 15 MINUTES

COOK TIME: 25 MINUTES

ACTIVE TIME: 25 MINUTES

TOTAL TIME: 40 MINUTES, PLUS COOLING AND CHILLING

COOK TEMPERATURE: 350°F

1. **For the crust:** Line a 7 × 3-inch round heatproof pan with foil, leaving a couple of inches of overhang. Spray the foil with vegetable oil spray.

2. In a medium bowl, combine the butter and brown sugar. Beat with an electric mixer on medium-low speed until light and fluffy. Add the flour and kosher salt and beat until the ingredients are well blended. Transfer the mixture (it will be crumbly) to the prepared pan. Press it evenly into the bottom of the pan.

3. Place the pan in the air fryer basket. Set the air fryer to 350°F for 13 minutes. When the crust has 5 minutes left to cook, start the filling.

4. **For the filling:** In a medium saucepan, combine the butter, brown sugar, maple syrup, and milk. Bring to a simmer, stirring occasionally. When it begins simmering, cook for 1 minute. Remove from the heat and stir in the vanilla and pecans.

5. Carefully pour the filling evenly over the crust, gently spreading with a rubber spatula so the nuts and liquid are evenly distributed. Set the air fryer to 350°F for 12 minutes, or until mixture is bubbling. (The center should still be slightly jiggly—it will thicken as it cools.)

6. Remove the pan from the air fryer and sprinkle the tart with the sea salt. Cool completely on a wire rack until room temperature.

7. Transfer the pan to the refrigerator to chill. When cold (the tart will be easier to cut), use the foil overhang to remove the tart from the pan and cut into 8 wedges. Serve at room temperature.

For the Tart Crust

Vegetable oil spray

⅓ cup (⅔ stick) butter, softened

¼ cup firmly packed brown sugar

1 cup all-purpose flour

¼ teaspoon kosher salt

For the Filling

4 tablespoons (½ stick) butter, diced

½ cup packed brown sugar

¼ cup pure maple syrup

¼ cup whole milk

¼ teaspoon pure vanilla extract

1½ cups finely chopped pecans

¼ teaspoon flaked sea salt

PEANUT BUTTER-HONEY-BANANA TOAST

EGG-FREE, SOY-FREE, VEGETARIAN

PREP TIME: 10 MINUTES

COOK TIME: 9 MINUTES

ACTIVE TIME: 10 MINUTES

TOTAL TIME: 19 MINUTES

COOK TEMPERATURE: 375°F/400°F

Think of this as a guide rather than a recipe with exact proportions. Basically, it's bread, buttered on one side, peanut buttered on the other side, then topped with bananas, honey, and cinnamon. YMMV on exactly how much of each ingredient you prefer. This is so delicious, especially with the slightly caramelized banana, that I really wish air fryers had been around when Elvis was alive, because if he loved the regular uncooked peanut butter–banana sandwich, he would have loved this!   **SERVINGS: 4**

- 2 tablespoons butter, softened
- 4 slices white bread
- 4 tablespoons peanut butter
- 2 bananas, peeled and thinly sliced
- 4 tablespoons honey
- 1 teaspoon ground cinnamon

1. Spread butter on one side of each slice of bread, then peanut butter on the other side. Arrange the banana slices on top of the peanut butter sides of each slice (about 9 slices per toast). Drizzle honey on top of the banana and sprinkle with cinnamon.

2. Cut each slice in half lengthwise so that it will better fit into the air fryer basket. Arrange two pieces of bread, butter sides down, in the air fryer basket. Set the air fryer to 375°F for 5 minutes. Then set the air fryer to 400°F for an additional 4 minutes, or until the bananas have started to brown. Repeat with remaining slices. Serve hot.

PICK-YOUR-FRUIT HAND PIES

I've given you the recipe with fresh dough, but refrigerated puff pastry also works well. With all the variations provided, you'll have a variety of ways to make these delicious desserts.   **SERVINGS: 2**

NUT-FREE, VEGETARIAN

PREP TIME: 25 MINUTES
COOK TIME: 8 MINUTES
ACTIVE TIME: 25 MINUTES
STANDING TIME: 20 MINUTES
TOTAL TIME: 55 MINUTES
COOK TEMPERATURE: 325°F

1. Preheat the air fryer to 325°F.

2. **For the pastry:** In a medium bowl, stir together the flour and salt. Using a pastry blender, cut in the shortening and butter until the pieces are pea-size. Sprinkle 1 tablespoon cold water over part of the flour mixture. Toss with a fork. Move the moistened pastry to the side of the bowl. Repeat with remaining flour, using 1 tablespoon of the water at a time, until everything is moist. Gather the flour mixture and knead gently only as much time as it takes to come together in a ball.

3. **For the pies:** On a lightly floured surface, slightly flatten the pastry, then roll from the center to the edge into a 13-inch circle. Place a 6-inch round baking pan on the pastry near one edge. Using a small, sharp knife, cut out a circle of pastry around the pan. Repeat to make two circles. Discard the dough scraps.

4. Place half of the fruit filling on half of one pastry circle, leaving a ¼-inch border. Brush the bare edge with water. Fold the empty half of the pastry over the filling. Using a fork, press around the edge of the pastry to seal it. Poke the top in a few places with a fork. Repeat with remaining filling and pastry.

5. In a small bowl, beat together the egg and water. Brush over the tops of the pies and sprinkle with the coarse sugar.

6. Place the pies in the air fryer basket. Set the air fryer to 325°F for 8 minutes, or until the pies are golden brown.

7. Cool the pies on a wire rack for at least 20 minutes before serving.

For the Pastry

- 1½ cups all-purpose flour
- ½ teaspoon kosher salt
- ¼ cup shortening
- ¼ cup ([½ stick]) butter, cut up
- ¼ to ⅓ cup cold water

For the Pies

- All-purpose flour
- Fruit Filling (see Variations, opposite)
- 1 large egg
- 1 tablespoon water
- 1 teaspoon coarse sugar

VARIATIONS

★ **Apple:** In a medium bowl, toss together ⅔ cup chopped apples, 1 tablespoon sugar, ½ teaspoon flour, and a dash of apple pie spice or cinnamon.

★ **Blueberry:** In a medium bowl, toss together ⅔ cup fresh blueberries, 3 tablespoons sugar, 1 teaspoon quick-cooking tapioca or cornstarch, and ½ teaspoon lemon zest.

★ **Cherry:** In a medium bowl, toss together ⅔ cup pitted tart cherries (thawed if frozen), ¼ cup sugar, and 1½ teaspoons quick cooking tapioca or cornstarch.

★ **Puff Pastry Method:** If you don't want to bother with your own pie crust, you can substitute puff pastry: On a lightly floured surface, roll a single sheet of thawed puff pastry (from a 17.3-ounce package) into a 13×7-inch rectangle, then cut out two 6-inch rounds as described above. Proceed with Step 4, cooking the puff pastry pies at 325°F for 20 minutes.

BANANAS FOSTER

Air-fried bananas are just divine. They cook fast, caramelize well, and make a lovely warm dessert. I usually skip the alcohol and flaming bit because I'm klutzy and I can just see myself burning off my eyebrows, but it does add a wonderful flavor.   **SERVINGS: 2**

GRAIN-FREE, GLUTEN-FREE, EGG-FREE, SOY-FREE, VEGETARIAN

PREP TIME: 5 MINUTES
COOK TIME: 7 MINUTES
ACTIVE TIME: 7 MINUTES
TOTAL TIME: 12 MINUTES
COOK TEMPERATURE: 350°F

1. In a 6 × 3-inch round heatproof pan, combine the butter and brown sugar. Place the pan in the air fryer basket. Set the air fryer to 350°F for 2 minutes, or until the butter and sugar are melted. Swirl to combine.

2. Add the banana pieces and pecans, turning the bananas to coat. Set the air fryer to 350°F for 5 minutes, turning the banana pieces halfway through the cooking time. Sprinkle with the cinnamon.

3. Remove the pan from the air fryer and place on an unlit stovetop for safety. Add the rum to the pan, swirling to combine it with the butter mixture. Carefully light the sauce with a long-reach lighter. Spoon the flaming sauce over the banana pieces until the flames die out.

4. Serve the warm bananas and sauce over vanilla ice cream.

- 1 tablespoon unsalted butter
- 2 teaspoons dark brown sugar
- 1 banana, peeled and halved lengthwise and then crosswise
- 2 tablespoons chopped pecans
- ⅛ teaspoon ground cinnamon
- 2 tablespoons light rum
- Vanilla ice cream, for serving

PUMPKIN-SPICE BREAD PUDDING WITH MAPLE-CREAM SAUCE

NUT-FREE, SOY-FREE, VEGETARIAN

PREP TIME: 15 MINUTES

COOK TIME: 35 MINUTES

ACTIVE TIME: 30 MINUTES

STANDING TIME: 10 MINUTES

TOTAL TIME: 1 HOUR

COOK TEMPERATURE: 350°F

Do not, I repeat, do *not* wait for Thanksgiving to make this bread pudding. Make it *all* the time because it is *so* good! That sauce—we had a hard time not eating it straight from the jar that I'd saved it in. And the pudding itself is super simple, super tasty, and very pretty to serve. Let everyone else enjoy the over-calorized pumpkin-spice lattes, it will be decadent bread pudding for you! **SERVINGS: 6**

1. **For the bread pudding:** In a medium bowl, combine the cream, pumpkin, milk, sugar, egg and yolk, pumpkin pie spice, and salt. Whisk until well combined.

2. In a large bowl, toss the bread cubes with the melted butter. Add the pumpkin mixture and gently toss until the ingredients are well combined.

3. Transfer the mixture to an ungreased 6 × 3-inch heatproof pan. Place the pan in the air fryer basket. Set the fryer to 350°F for 35 minutes, or until custard is set in the middle.

4. **Meanwhile, for the sauce:** In a small saucepan, combine the syrup and butter. Heat over medium heat, stirring, until the butter melts. Stir in the cream and simmer, stirring often, until the sauce has thickened, about 15 minutes. Stir in the vanilla. Remove the pudding from the air fryer.

5. Let the pudding stand for 10 minutes before serving with the warm sauce.

For the Bread Pudding

- ¾ cup heavy whipping cream
- ½ cup canned pumpkin
- ⅓ cup whole milk
- ⅓ cup sugar
- 1 large egg plus 1 yolk
- ½ teaspoon pumpkin pie spice
- ⅛ teaspoon kosher salt
- 4 cups 1-inch cubed day-old baguette or crusty country bread
- 4 tablespoons (½ stick) unsalted butter, melted

For the Sauce

- ⅓ cup pure maple syrup
- 1 tablespoon unsalted butter
- ½ cup heavy whipping cream
- ½ teaspoon pure vanilla extract

SPICED APPLE CAKE

The nutmeg in this cake is what makes it different from other spice cakes, and oh, that is such a delightful difference! The combination of apples with the nutmeg and other spices, all mixed into a buttery batter, is just perfect.   **SERVINGS: 6**

1. Grease a 3-cup Bundt pan with oil; set aside.

2. In a medium bowl, toss the apples with the lemon juice until well coated; set aside.

3. In a large bowl, combine the butter and sugar. Beat with an electric hand mixer on medium speed until the sugar has dissolved. Add the eggs and beat until fluffy. Add the flour, baking powder, apple pie spice, ginger, cardamom, nutmeg, salt, and milk. Mix until the batter is thick but pourable.

4. Pour the batter into the prepared pan. Top batter evenly with the apple mixture. Place the pan in the air fryer basket. Set the air fryer to 350°F for 30 minutes, or until a toothpick inserted in the center of the cake comes out clean. Close the air fryer and let the cake rest for 10 minutes. Turn the cake out onto a wire rack and cool completely.

5. Right before serving, dust the cake with confectioners' sugar.

NUT-FREE, SOY-FREE, VEGETARIAN

PREP TIME: 15 MINUTES
COOK TIME: 30 MINUTES
ACTIVE TIME: 15 MINUTES
STANDING TIME: 10 MINUTES
TOTAL TIME: 55 MINUTES PLUS COOLING
COOK TEMPERATURE: 350°F

Vegetable oil

2 cups diced peeled Gala apples (about 2 apples)

1 tablespoon fresh lemon juice

¼ cup (½ stick) unsalted butter, softened

⅓ cup granulated sugar

2 large eggs

1¼ cups unbleached all-purpose flour

1½ teaspoons baking powder

1 tablespoon apple pie spice

½ teaspoon ground ginger

¼ teaspoon ground cardamom

¼ teaspoon ground nutmeg

½ teaspoon kosher salt

¼ cup whole milk

Confectioners' sugar, for dusting

SPICE

MIXES

CAJUN SPICE MIX

You can certainly use a store-bought Cajun mix, but I like making it at home so that I can play with the proportions. I like to add more cayenne than what I have listed here, so you can always use more (or less!) than the 1 teaspoon.   **MAKES: ½ CUP**

1. In a clean coffee grinder or spice mill, combine all the spices and process to a moderately fine powder.

2. Unplug the grinder and turn it upside down. (You want all the ground spices to collect in the lid so you can easily scoop them out without cutting yourself on the blades.) Store in an airtight container in a cool, dark place for up to 2 months.

PREP TIME: 10 MINUTES
ACTIVE TIME: 10 MINUTES
TOTAL TIME: 10 MINUTES

- 1 tablespoon dried parsley
- 1 tablespoon dehydrated onion flakes
- 1 tablespoon smoked paprika
- 1 teaspoon dried oregano
- 1 teaspoon dried thyme
- 1 teaspoon cayenne pepper
- 1 teaspoon garlic powder
- 1 teaspoon kosher salt
- 1 teaspoon black pepper

GARAM MASALA

If you own any of my other cookbooks, you know I swear by this garam masala recipe—and you also know that I *insist* you make it fresh, from whole seeds, and in small batches. Listen, I'm all about shortcuts. If I tell you to make your own rather than buy it? There's a good reason. #TrustUrvashi **MAKES: ¼ CUP**

1. In a clean coffee grinder or spice mill, combine all the spices and grind, shaking so all the seeds and bits get into the blades, until the mixture has the consistency of a moderately fine powder.

2. Unplug the grinder and turn it upside down. (You want all the ground spices to collect in the lid so you can easily scoop them out without cutting yourself on the blades.) Store in an airtight container in a cool, dark place for up to 2 months.

PREP TIME: 10 MINUTES
ACTIVE TIME: 10 MINUTES
TOTAL TIME: 10 MINUTES

- 2 tablespoons coriander seeds
- 1 teaspoon cumin seeds
- ½ teaspoon whole black cloves
- ½ teaspoon cardamom seeds
- 2 dried bay leaves
- 3 dried red chiles; or ½ teaspoon cayenne pepper or red pepper flakes
- 1 (2-inch) piece cinnamon stick

SPICE MIXES

HARISSA

Many harissa recipes use tomatoes or peppers. I prefer my paste to be straight-up spice. Taste it once and you will find a million different uses for this lovely, spicy, versatile mix.   **MAKES: 1 CUP**

PREP TIME: 5 MINUTES
COOK TIME: 5 MINUTE
ACTIVE TIME: 5 MINUTES
TOTAL TIME: 10 MINUTES
COOK TEMPERATURE: 350°F

1. In a medium microwave-safe bowl, combine all the ingredients. Microwave on high for 1 minute, stirring halfway through the cooking time. (You can also heat this on the stovetop until the oil is hot and bubbling. Or, if you must use your air fryer for everything, cook in the air fryer at 350°F for 5 to 6 minutes, or until the paste is heated through.)

2. Cool completely. Store in an airtight container in the refrigerator for up to 1 month.

½ cup olive oil

6 cloves garlic, minced

2 tablespoons smoked paprika

1 tablespoon ground coriander

1 tablespoon ground cumin

1 teaspoon ground caraway

1 teaspoon kosher salt

½ to 1 teaspoon cayenne pepper

LEBANESE SEVEN-SPICE MIX

Every Lebanese family has their own version of seven-spice mix. Since I am not Lebanese, I do not, sadly, have a secret family recipe to share with you. What I *do* have is a mix that I make often, and that works for me. Here's hoping you enjoy it too! And if you do have a family recipe? Come join my Facebook group and share it with the rest of us!   **MAKES: ⅓ CUP**

In a small bowl, stir together all the ingredients. Store in an airtight container in a cool, dark place for up to 2 months.

PREP TIME: 5 MINUTES
ACTIVE TIME: 5 MINUTES
TOTAL TIME: 5 MINUTES

- 1 tablespoon ground allspice
- 1 tablespoon ground cloves
- 1 tablespoon grated nutmeg
- 1 tablespoon ground fenugreek
- 1 tablespoon ground ginger
- 2 teaspoons ground cinnamon
- 2 teaspoons black pepper

NIGERIAN SUYA SPICE MIX

GRAIN-FREE, GLUTEN-FREE,
EGG-FREE, SOY-FREE,
DAIRY-FREE, VEGAN,
LOW-CARB

I am a peanut fan. I have yet to meet a peanut in a form I couldn't appreciate. Boiled, roasted, raw, whole, crushed—bring it all. But peanuts in a spice mix? I mean really, does it get more perfect? I love this with the flank steak (page 144), but I often use it on steamed, buttered vegetables to add a little kick to them. **MAKES: ½ CUP**

PREP TIME: 10 MINUTES
ACTIVE TIME: 10 MINUTES
TOTAL TIME: 10 MINUTES

- ¼ cup dry-roasted peanuts
- 1 teaspoon cumin seeds
- 1 teaspoon garlic powder
- 1 teaspoon smoked paprika
- ½ teaspoon ground ginger
- 1 teaspoon kosher salt
- ½ teaspoon cayenne pepper

1. In a clean coffee grinder or spice mill, combine the peanuts and cumin seeds. Process until you get a coarse powder. (Do not over-process or you will wind up with peanut butter! Alternatively, you can grind the cumin with ⅓ cup ready-made peanut powder, such as PB2, instead of the peanuts.)

2. Pour the peanut mixture into a small bowl, add the garlic powder, paprika, ginger, salt, and cayenne, and stir to combine.

3. Store in an airtight container in a cool, dark place for up to 2 months.

RAS AL HANOUT

Once again, recipes for this heady mix vary family by family, and shop by shop, since the name simply means "top of the shop," or the best of what the shop has to offer. When I'm feeling extravagant, I add liberal amounts of saffron, but most days I find the recipe below to be just right for us.   **MAKES: ⅓ CUP**

In a small bowl, stir together all the ingredients. Store in an airtight container in a cool, dark place for up to 2 months.

PREP TIME: 5 MINUTES
ACTIVE TIME: 5 MINUTES
TOTAL TIME: 5 MINUTES

- 2 teaspoons ground cumin
- 2 teaspoons ground ginger
- 2 teaspoons ground turmeric
- 1 teaspoon ground cardamom
- 1 teaspoon ground cinnamon
- 1 teaspoon ground coriander
- 1 teaspoon cayenne pepper
- 1 teaspoon ground allspice
- 2 teaspoons kosher salt
- 2 teaspoons black pepper

SOUTH INDIAN PEPPER SPICE MIX

Did you know that I also conduct culinary tours in various countries? (Basically, just an excuse to eat, shop, and learn how to cook, really.) We recently led a tour in South India where the food was utterly delectable. In this spice mix, I tried to reproduce the basic flavors of a pepper chicken fry. Use as your imagination directs, without limiting yourself to traditional options! **MAKES: 3 TABLESPOONS**

1½ teaspoons coriander seeds

1 teaspoon fennel seeds

1 teaspoon cumin seeds

1 teaspoon black peppercorns

½ teaspoon cardamom seeds

1 dried red chile, or ½ teaspoon dried red pepper flakes

1 1-inch piece cinnamon stick

¼ teaspoon ground turmeric

1 teaspoon kosher salt

1. In a clean coffee grinder or spice mill, combine the coriander, fennel, cumin, peppercorns, cardamom, dried chile, and cinnamon stick. Grind, shaking the grinder lightly so all the seeds and bits get into the blades, until the mixture is broken down to moderately fine powder. Stir in the turmeric and salt.

2. Store in an airtight container in a cool, dark place for up to 2 months.

CHART OF DIETARY CONSIDERATIONS AND COOKING TIMES

RECIPES	PAGE	DAIRY-FREE	EGG-FREE	GLUTEN-FREE	GRAIN-FREE	LOW-CARB
BACON-WRAPPED PICKLE SPEARS	2		X	X	X	X
CARAMELIZED ONION DIP	3		X	X	X	X
CHEESE DROPS	4		X			
LEBANESE MUHAMMARA	7	X	X	X	X	X
MASALA PEANUTS	8	X	X	X	X	X
ONION PAKORAS	10	X	X	X		X
PEPPERONI PIZZA DIP	11		X	X	X	X
PIGS IN PUFF-PASTRY BLANKETS	12					
SAVORY POTATO PATTIES	15	X	X	X	X	
SMOKY HAM & CHEESE PARTY BISCUITS	17		X			
SMOKY SALMON DIP	19		X	X	X	X
SMOKY EGGPLANT TAHINI DIP	20	X	X	X	X	X
CHEESY BAKED GRITS	24			X		
HARISSA SHAKSHUKA	27	X		X	X	X
INDIAN MASALA OMELET	28	X		X	X	X
QUESO FUNDIDO	29		X	X	X	X
SWEET & SAVORY TRIANGLES	30		X			
TOAD IN THE HOLE	32					
CHEESY HAM & POTATOES RACLETTE	33		X	X	X	
BLISTERED SHISHITO PEPPERS WITH SOUR CREAM DIPPING SAUCE	37	X	X	X	X	X
CHERMOULA-ROASTED BEETS	38	X	X	X	X	X
CHILE-CHEESE CORNBREAD WITH CORN	41					
CRISPY SESAME-GINGER BROCCOLI	42	X	X	X	X	X
FRIED PLANTAINS	45	X	X	X	X	
GREEN BEANS & BACON	46	X	X	X	X	X
MEXICAN CORN IN A CUP	49			X		
CREAMED SPINACH	50		X	X	X	X
MUSHROOMS WITH GOAT CHEESE	51		X	X	X	X
PASTA WITH MASCARPONE MUSHROOMS	53		X	X	X	X
RADISHES O'BRIEN	54	X	X	X	X	X
RAS AL HANOUT-ROASTED CARROTS WITH HARISSA SOUR CREAM	57		X	X	X	
ROASTED CAULIFLOWER WITH CILANTRO-JALAPEÑO SAUCE	58		X	X	X	X
ROASTED RATATOUILLE	61	X	X	X	X	X
ROSEMARY & CHEESE-ROASTED RED POTATOES	62		X	X	X	
SPICED BUTTERNUT SQUASH	65	X	X	X	X	
SPICED GLAZED CARROTS	66	X	X	X	X	
SPINACH & CHEESE-STUFFED TOMATOES	70		X	X	X	X
RUSSET & SWEET POTATO GRATIN	71		X	X	X	
SWEET POTATO FRIES WITH AJI CRIOLLO MAYO	73	X		X	X	
SWEET & CRISPY ROASTED PEARL ONIONS	74	X	X	X	X	X
ZUCCHINI & TOMATO SALAD	75	X	X	X	X	X
BACON-WRAPPED STUFFED CHICKEN BREASTS	78		X	X	X	X
CHICKEN CORDON BLEU	79			X	X	X
BRAZILIAN TEMPERO BAIANO CHICKEN DRUMSTICKS	80	X	X	X	X	X
CHICKEN JALFREZI	83	X	X	X	X	X
CILANTRO CHICKEN KEBABS	84	X	X	X	X	X
CRISPY INDONESIAN CHICKEN WINGS	87	X	X			X
CURRY MUSTARD CHICKEN	89	X		X	X	X
FRENCH GARLIC CHICKEN	90		X	X	X	X
GINGER CHICKEN	92	X	X			X
HARISSA-RUBBED CORNISH GAME HENS	93		X	X	X	X
LEBANESE TURKEY BURGERS WITH FETA & TZATZIKI	95		X	X	X	X

NUT-FREE	PALEO	SOY-FREE	VEGETARIAN	VEGAN	30 MIN OR LESS	COOK TIME	TOTAL TIME	TEMPERATURE (in °F)
X		X			X	8	18	400
X		X	X			30	2 HR 40	200/375
X		X	X			20	35	325
	X	X	X	X	X	15	30	400
		X	X	X		15	40	325/400
X		X	X	X		20	1 HR	350
X		X			X	10	20	350
X		X				16	30-40	350
X		X	X	X		10	35	400
X		X				16	40	400
		X			X	7	17	400
X		X	X	X		15	45	400
X		X	X		X	12	22	400
X	X	X	X		X	15	30	350
X	X	X	X		X	12	22	250
X		X				25	35	400/325
X		X				20	35	400
X		X				35	45	400/350
II		A				25	35	400
X		X	X		X	6	11	400
X	X	X	X	X		25	40	375
X		X	X			15	35	350
X		X	X	X	X	15	25	325
X		X	X	X	X	8	18	400
X		X				20	35	375/400
X		X	X		X	10	15	350
X		X	X		X	15	25	350/400
X		X	X		X	10	20	400
X		X	X		X	15	25	350
X	X	X	X	X		23	33	350/400
X		X	X		X	12	22	400
X		X	X			20	35	400
X	X	X	X	X		20	35	400
X		X	X		X	15	25	400
X		X	X	X	X	15	25	400
X		X	X	X		30	40	400
X		X	X			15	35	350
X		X	X			45	1 HR 5	350/400
X	X	X	X		X	20	30	400
X	X	X	X	X	X	18	23	400
X		X	X	X	X	10	20	400
X		X				30	45	350
X		X				25	40	350
X	X	X				20	55	400
X	X	X				15	35	350
X	X	X				10	45	350
X		X				25	40	400
X	X	X			X	15	25	350
X		X				27	1 HR 15	400/350
X						10	50	350
X		X				21	60	400
X		X				12	37	400

(continued)

RECIPES	PAGE	DAIRY-FREE	EGG-FREE	GLUTEN-FREE	GRAIN-FREE	LOW-CARB
ONE-DISH CHICKEN & RICE	96	X	X	X		
PEANUT CHICKEN	97	X	X			X
SOUTH INDIAN PEPPER CHICKEN	99	X	X	X	X	X
PESTO CREAM CHICKEN WITH CHERRY TOMATOES	100		X	X	X	X
SPICY ROAST CHICKEN	101	X	X	X	X	X
BANG BANG SHRIMP	105	X		X		
CAJUN FRIED SHRIMP WITH REMOULADE	107			X		X
CHILEAN SEA BASS WITH OLIVE RELISH	108	X	X	X	X	X
CHINESE GINGER-SCALLION FISH	109	X	X			X
GARLIC PEANUT SHRIMP	110	X	X	X	X	X
GREEN CURRY SHRIMP	113		X			X
ONE-POT SHRIMP FRIED RICE	115	X				
SALMON CROQUETTES	116	X		X	X	X
PESTO FISH PIE	118		X			
SOUTH INDIAN FRIED FISH	119	X	X	X	X	X
TANDOORI SHRIMP	121	X	X	X	X	X
SCALLOPS GRATINÉ WITH PARMESAN	122		X	X	X	X
BAKED KIBBEH	127	X	X			
CAJUN BACON PORK LOIN FILET	129	X	X	X	X	X
BULGOGI BEEF	130	X	X			X
CHIPOTLE STEAK TACOS	132		X	X	X	X
CURRYWURST	131	X	X	X	X	X
GERMAN ROULADEN-STYLE STEAK	134		X	X	X	X
HAM, CHICKEN & CHEESE CASSEROLE	135		X	X	X	X
ITALIAN STEAK ROLLS	136		X	X	X	X
KHEEMA BURGERS	137			X	X	X
KOREAN BEEF TACOS	140	X	X			X
MONTREAL STEAK BURGERS	141	X				X
LAMB CHOPS WITH HORSERADISH SAUCE	143	X		X	X	X
NIGERIAN PEANUT-CRUSTED FLANK STEAK	144	X	X	X	X	X
PHILLY CHEESESTEAKS	147		X			
PORCHETTA-STYLE PORK CHOPS	149	X	X	X	X	X
SPICY CHICKEN-FRIED STEAK WITH PEPPERCORN GRAVY	150					
SPICY FLANK STEAK WITH ZHOUG	153	X	X		X	X
SWEET & SPICY COUNTRY-STYLE RIBS	155	X	X	X	X	
POBLANO CHEESEBURGERS WITH AVOCADO-CHIPOTLE MAYO	156			X	X	X
TACO MEATBALLS	158			X	X	X
WONTON MEATBALLS	159	X				X
APPLE DUTCH BABY	163					
BLUEBERRY-CREAM CHEESE BREAD PUDDING	165					
SPICED PEARS WITH HONEY-LEMON RICOTTA	166		X	X	X	
INDIAN TOAST & MILK	169					
MAPLE-PECAN TART WITH SEA SALT	170		X			
PEANUT BUTTER-HONEY-BANANA TOAST	173		X			
PICK-YOUR-FRUIT HAND PIES	174					
BANANAS FOSTER	176		X	X	X	
PUMPKIN-SPICE BREAD PUDDING WITH MAPLE-CREAM SAUCE	177					
SPICED APPLE CAKE	178					
CAJUN SPICE MIX	182	X	X	X	X	X
GARAM MASALA	183	X	X	X	X	X
HARISSA	184	X	X	X	X	X
LEBANESE SEVEN-SPICE MIX	186	X	X	X	X	X
NIGERIAN SUYA SPICE MIX	187	X	X	X	X	X
RAS AL HANOUT	188	X	X	X	X	X
SOUTH INDIAN PEPPER SPICE MIX	189	X	X	X	X	X

NUT-FREE	PALEO	SOY-FREE	VEGETARIAN	VEGAN	30 MIN OR LESS	COOK TIME	TOTAL TIME	TEMPERATURE (in °F)
X		X				40	50	375/400
						20	1 HR 5	350
X	X	X				15	1 HR 5	350/400
		X			X	15	25	350
X	X	X				10	50	350
X		X			X	14	30	350
X		X				8	53	350
X	X	X			X	10	20	325
X					X	15	30	350
		X			X	10	30	400/350
X						5	35	400
X						25	35	350
X	X				X	15	25	400
		X				15	35	400
X		X			X	8	30	325/400
X	X	X				6	35	325
X		X			X	9	20	325/400
		X				28	43	400/350
X	X					20	1 HR 40	350/400
X						12	52	400
X		X				8	53	400
X	X	X			X	15	27	400
X		X				15	45	400
X		X			X	15	30	350
X		X				9	1 HR 10	400
X		X			X	12	27	350
X						12	52	400
X	X	X			X	10	20	350
X		X				13	53	325/400
		X				8	53	400
X						20	40	400
	X				X	15	25	375
X		X				8	45	400
X		X				8	1 HR 30	400
X		X				25	35	350
X		X				27	60	375/350
X		X			X	10	25	400
X					X	10	25	350
X		X	X			16	1 HR 6	400/350
x		x	x			70	1 hr 35	400/350
		X	X		X	8	20	375
X		X	X			20	60	350
		X	X			25	40	350
		X	X		X	9	19	375/400
X			X			8	55	325
		X	X		X	7	12	350
X		X	X			35	60	350
X		X	X			30	55	350
X	X	X	X	X	X		10	
X	X	X	X	X	X		10	
X	X	X	X	X	X	5	10	350
X	X	X	X	X	X		5	
		X	X	X	X		10	
X	X	X	X	X	X		5	
X	X	X	X	X	X		10	

INDEX

Note: Page references in *italics* indicate photographs

AIR FRYER REVOLUTION

Make More Amazing Air Fryer Meals with

★ EVERY DAY EASY ★
AIR FRYER
100 RECIPES BURSTING WITH FLAVOR

URVASHI PITRE

BBQ CHICKEN FLATBREADS

CARNE ASADA

GLUTEN-FREE CHOCOLATE CAKE